Julian Baggini is the Founding Editor of *The Philosophers' Magazine*. His books include *Welcome to Everytown: A Journey into the English Mind*, *What's It All About? Philosophy and the Meaning of Life*, the bestselling *The Pig That Wants to be Eaten* and *Do They Think You're Stupid?*, all published by Granta Books.

THE EGO TRICK

Julian Baggini

GRANTA

Granta Publications, 12 Addison Avenue, London W11 4QR

First published in Great Britain by Granta Books 2011
This edition published by Granta Books 2012

A CIP catalogue record for this book
is available from the British Library.

5 7 9 10 8 6 4

ISBN 978 1 84708 273 2

Typeset in Bembo by M Rules

Printed and bound by CPI Group (UK) Ltd, Croydon, CR0 4YY

For Antonia, *la mia vera anima gemella*,
with love and gratitude

For my part, when I enter most intimately into what I call *myself*, I always stumble on some particular perception or other, of heat or cold, light or shade, love or hatred, pain or pleasure, colour or sound, etc. I never catch *myself*, distinct from some such perception.

David Hume, *Treatise of Human Nature*,
Book 1, Part 4, Section 6

Why, look you now, how unworthy a thing you make of me! You would play upon me; you would seem to know my stops; you would pluck out the heart of my mystery; you would sound me from my lowest note to the top of my compass: and there is much music, excellent voice, in this little organ; yet cannot you make it speak. 'Sblood, do you think I am easier to be played on than a pipe?

William Shakespeare, *Hamlet*, Act 3, Scene 2

Contents

Introduction

A seven-year-old boy has a ball roughly wrestled from him by an aggressive older schoolmate during an exuberant game of no-rules football. Enraged, he sees a block of wood within arm's reach, filling the square hole in the ground where goalposts usually stand. What happens next feels less like an action the child performs and more like something his body does of its own accord. With the older boy walking away, his back turned, the aggrieved kid finds himself picking up the wood and hurling it at his rival, hitting him on the back of the head. For a few seconds, it is as though he is not himself. It is the only act of violence in his life so far, and will remain so for at least the next thirty-five years.

A seventy-year-old man is sitting in a chair in a care home. The woman talking to him is the love of his life, someone he had lived with for thirty-two years. But he doesn't recognise her. Nor does he have any idea that the books she is holding are ones that he himself wrote. He wouldn't now be able to understand even a word of them.

A 42-year-old man is sitting on a train, typing these words. The boy's story belongs to his past, the old man's to his possible future. Yet looking backwards and forwards, unable to recognise himself in either child or pensioner, he finds he cannot answer an apparently simple question: was that boy and would that man be *me*?

Some may be puzzled by this puzzlement. *Of course* all three people are the same. Each is a stage in the life of a single human organism, one which carries the unique DNA of a person identified as Julian Baggini. Certainly, each is different, but this simply reflects the banal truism that *people change*. When we say 'I am no longer the same person', that's just a figure of speech. To take it more literally would be to make the classic philosophical mistake, identified by Wittgenstein, of becoming 'bewitched by language'.

I don't think this question or others like it can be dismissed as simply as that. Such puzzles of identity are not merely games philosophers play, they are lived out in the lives of real people every day. Most strikingly, they arise when people have to come to terms with loved ones suffering from dementia, damaged by some forms of severe brain injury, or in a permanent vegetative state. People talk about a time in the past when such people 'were still with us' even as their physical presence suggests they still are. Often, by the time the body finally gives up its last breath, the mourning for the person has already largely been done. How can this be possible unless, in a very real sense, we are not simply the same as the biological organisms that carry our DNA, and our personal identity is something that can diverge from the life of the body we inhabit?

And yet, the same people who mourn for loved ones before clinical death do not, on the whole, cease to care for the damaged selves oblivious in their care homes or strapped to life-support machines. There is another equally real sense in which, even in such a lamentable state, the persons that remain are the very same persons that, in another sense, we believe no longer exist.

This is only one of a cluster of what might be called 'paradoxes of the self': beliefs we have about who and what we are which have an equal force yet which contradict one another. To call them paradoxes, however, is to be too pessimistic about our ability to reconcile their conflicting claims. It is better to think of them as riddles to be solved. Our ideas about who we are may well pull in opposite directions, but I believe that more than two millennia of philosophy and over a century of psychology have provided us with the resources we need to show that the truths in both do not cancel out, but complete each other.

The central riddle I've set out to solve concerns the self's continuity in change: how can we remain the same people over time, even as we change, sometimes considerably? Dementia is perhaps the most extreme real-life example, but most of us can get some sense of the riddle's force simply by trying to remember how we were in the past. How often do we cringe when we come across things we wrote as teenagers, or are reminded of what we once said or did by others who were there? For instance, I remember my mother finding the words to a rude song a friend and I had written, one which was not only vulgar but based on such complete gynaecological ignorance I can't bring myself to tell you more about it, even now. Such acute embarrassment would only make sense if I felt that this was something I had myself done. But at the same time, the reason I feel embarrassed is precisely because of the disconnect between the man I believe myself to be and the child whose mind I can no longer get inside. I know I did it, but I cannot recapture a feeling for the me who did do it. Can most of us truly recall what it was really like to be five, ten or thirteen years old? The older we get, the less able we are to identify truly, with confidence, with our past selves. Sometimes, especially looking back on emotional traumas, we cannot explain what we did and thought only a few years ago. Our thoughts and actions are as inscrutable as those of strangers, or more so.

At the same time, each of us has a sense of 'me-ness' which appears to be remarkably enduring, and which can assert itself in unexpected ways. For example, I recently met up with a group of old university friends, some of whom I'd seen hardly at all for twenty years. Yet instantly, we were all completely at ease, recognising precisely those same features in each other we had come to know so well while sharing a house. Indeed, it was slightly depressing afterwards to realise how little we had changed. I liked to think I had grown and matured as a person, but whatever growth there had been seemed insignificant compared to what had not changed about me at all.

It seems that, over time, we change completely, yet remain completely the same. These inconsistencies in how we relate to past selves were captured lucidly by the film director Luis Buñuel in his autobiography. 'My lifetime often seems to me like an instant. Events in my childhood sometimes seem so recent that I have to make an effort to remember that they happened fifty or sixty years ago,' he wrote. 'And yet at other times life seems to me very long. The child, or the young man, who did this or that doesn't seem to have anything to do with me anymore.'[1]

There is a wealth of scholarly work in philosophy, psychology and neuroscience that can help us solve such riddles. However, too much of the brilliant literature on this subject is written by specialists in ways that conceal – sometimes it seems wilfully – their wider interest. Specialisation also disguises the extent to which philosophy, psychology, sociology, neuroscience and religion have different approaches, but all converge on the same subject. Academics in these fields often seem like critics each discussing a different detail of a painting, not realising they are all talking about the same picture. My aim is to step back and try to see this broader canvas. This should not, however, mean dispensing with rigour: a broad brush needs to be handled with as much care as a fine nib.

To regain the sense in which these issues touch all our lives, I have relied not just on books and theories, but also encounters with people who in various ways live out many of the issues that academics merely theorise about. To get an insight into the meaning of reincarnation, I've spoken to Buddhist lamas with claims to past lives. To investigate the importance of our bodies for identity, I've met people who have changed gender. To better understand how dementia affects who we are, I've talked with people who have seen loved ones transformed by the disease. Such authentic encounters provide more than just vivid examples of what the theoreticians talk about; they can help clarify the difficult conceptual issues themselves. They also remind us that this is not just an abstract, academic concern, but a real issue that affects real lives, something I hope the portraits that appear as interludes between chapters reinforce.

Dealing with these issues is complicated by the fact that the question of personal identity comes in a bewildering number of forms. Some take it to be an issue in empirical psychology as to what in nature or nurture forms us into the distinct personalities we are. Others assume the question is a social one: what are the ethnic, religious and social identities which we ascribe to ourselves and others to define who we are? A minority take the central issue to be the one that was the subject of my PhD: what are the necessary and sufficient conditions for saying that a person at one time is the same as a person at another? No wonder that there are so many different ways of understanding the issue: two psychologists recently catalogued sixty-six different terms for aspects of self and identity.[2]

What the existence of these differing responses shows is that although the very meaning of identity implies unity and oneness, the identity of selves is actually about many things. But while it may make sense to separate these questions for certain forms of specialised academic enquiry, a comprehensive account of what we are has to address all of them to a lesser or greater extent. My question – which I think is the question that is of most interest to most people – is a broad one: what are we and on what does our continued existence over time depend? This breadth also means that I do not think I have to specify in advance whether my subject is persons, individuals, human beings or selves, as academics are often obliged to do. I will simply use each of these concepts appropriately as they relate to the central question.

The Irish philosopher Bishop Berkeley once wrote, 'Philosophers have raised a dust and then complain that they cannot see.' The cloud that obscures our view of the self has been thickened by the trampling of psychologists, scientists, theologians and sociologists too. In contemporary academia, the assumed solution to this often seems to be that we should examine each particle of dirt in ever more isolated detail. My approach is rather to let the dust settle and have another close look at what it is that everyone was stampeding to see. Selves are like paintings: they cannot be brought into focus if you stand too far away or too close. Viewed properly, we will see that selves are real, but they are not what most of us imagine them to be.

PART ONE

Pearl Diving

Do you have an essential 'you-ness'? When asked, most people say they do, but I've yet to meet anyone who can explain clearly what this 'me-ness' is. People may describe it as a kind of ever-present 'feeling', a sense that is always there in the background, or perhaps even as a kind of 'flavour' that runs through all their experiences. Although people recognise that they have changed enormously since they were children, most claim that, nonetheless, their sense of 'me-ness' has remained constant.

Whether we are right to believe in such an essence is a question I hope will be answered by the end of this book. For now, however, what is significant is simply that people almost invariably believe that there is such an essence, a core of self that holds steady through life. This is sometimes called the 'pearl' view. The problem is that no one seems to be quite sure where to locate this precious gem. If everyone does have an enduring essence, something which makes them the same person throughout their lives, and perhaps even after it, then where and what is it?

'*I feel like I've lived several lifetimes these days. It's very weird to look back at my childhood and have a sense of that being me.*'

Jñanamitra, who has lived as a man and as a woman

1

Bodies of thought

Before embarking on any search for an elusive entity, it is prudent to first check that what you're looking for isn't already right under your nose. In the case of the self, there are some who would urge us to look above and behind it too. When you try to establish the identity of another person, or to prove your own, there is never any existential or metaphysical mystery. Rather, you show your passport or your driving licence, you give a fingerprint, take a blood test, or have your DNA read. Identify the body and you identify the person.

In practical terms, there is no deep puzzle about our identity. We receive certificates of birth and death and there is rarely any difficulty in matching the two. As the contemporary philosopher Eric T. Olsen puts it, 'Isn't it obvious that we are animals?'[1] So obvious, in fact, that if you consider the alternatives, you'll find that 'No one but a philosopher could have thought of them. And it would take quite a bit of philosophy to get anyone to believe one of them. Compared with these claims, the idea that we are animals looks downright sensible.'

Olsen sounds almost embarrassed to have to defend the view called animalism, which is simply the claim that 'there is a certain human organism, and that organism is you. You and it are one and the same.' This does not mean that we are 'merely' animals. We are other things as well, such as philosophers, musicians, gardeners or anarchists. 'We may be very special animals,' says Olsen. 'But special animals are still animals.'

This point is worth stressing. One of the cheapest and most effective rhetorical tricks in the book is the use of the debunking 'just' or 'mere'. Many perfectly sound ideas can be made to appear quite implausible by the judicious insertion of one of these words. Critics deny that thought is 'merely' the product of brain function, that human beings are 'just' biological machines, or that music is 'nothing more than' the vibration of air. Take away the words in scare-quotes, however, and what is so outrageous about any of these statements?

The idea, therefore, that what makes us the individuals we are is that we are particular biological organisms should not be dismissed on the grounds that we do much more than eat and reproduce. If we are animals, we are clearly quite remarkable ones, and no animalist would suggest otherwise.

In some sense, Olsen is right that we are obviously animals. However, is it true that this is where we find the core of self, the elusive pearl of identity? It is one thing to say that we need bodies to live, another to say that it is our bodies which define who we are. The fact that bodies are essential does not mean they define our essences.

Philosophers' and novelists' thought experiments about people switching bodies challenge the idea that we are simply our bodies. John Locke imagined the mind and soul of a prince entering that of a cobbler,[2] while in *Metamorphosis*, Franz Kafka imagined a man waking up with the body of a beetle. These fantasies do not, of course, show that such transformations are possible. However, that they are imaginable, and that we intuitively think that the prince and the man continued to live on in their strange, new bodies, reflects a strong sense we have that our essence is not to be found in our original biological casings. The distinction between the thinking person within and the animal vehicle for its continued existence is one that even a child can make, without any philosophical coaching.

However, there are good reasons to be suspicious of how much mere fictions like this can tell us. The fact that we can imagine something does not prove that it is possible. I can imagine myself running a mile in ten seconds, but I could never do it. Worse, sometimes we believe we have successfully imagined something when we have in fact done no such thing. Take another of John Locke's thought experiments, where he asks us to imagine what would happen if you cut off your little finger, and consciousness went with this finger, not the rest of the body left behind. 'It is evident the little finger would be the person, the same person,' he wrote, 'and self then would have nothing to do with the rest of the body.' That sounds reasonable. But if you think about it, what on earth would it mean for a little finger to be a conscious person? Can you really imagine what it is like to be a digit-person?

Fortunately, we do not have to reply on imagination alone to help us make sense of the importance of our biological bodies for identity. We have real-life cases of people who, dissatisfied with their own bodies, change them radically. I'm not talking here about cosmetic surgery, but the far deeper changes that are made when a person transitions from one gender to another. If being in a particular body really is essential to our identity, then transgendered men and women should be able to tell us something about how and why this is so.

Living in the wrong body

Drusilla Marland knows something about how difficult it can be for even good friends to understand what leads a person to change gender, because one of her friends, Richard Beard, wrote a wonderfully frank book about it. On its first page, he describes what he was thinking when he first saw the camping companion he had known for years as Andrew in pearl earrings: 'You are a 43-year-old man whose wife has just left you for another bloke, taking your daughter with her. You have a dismantled crankcase on the table in your front room. You drink lunchtime pints of Smiles Old Tosser and you work in the engine room of a 7,000 ton passenger ship. You are not a woman.'[3]

Marland certainly looked like a woman when I met her in her Bristol home. The same was true of Jñanamitra, another man who had transitioned to woman, whom I met for coffee in a Birmingham shopping centre. Jñanamitra adopted her name when she became 'ordained' in the Friends of the Western Buddhist Order, as they call becoming a full member. By that time she had lived as a man, as a not fully transitioned woman, and then as a man again. But she was lucky: Jñanamitra is an androgynous name she could take with her when she finally became a woman.

Changing gender is not straightforward. 'The major public mis-apprehension with transexualism is that you go into hospital, you have an operation and you come out a woman,' Jñanamitra explained to me. 'It's never been like that and it isn't like that. What happens really is a second puberty, where with the hormone treatment, over several years, your body gradually changes, more to be the form you feel yourself to be.'

Indeed, it is such a difficult process that for many years doctors would use hormones as a diagnostic tool, to see if the client really did want to change gender. In the seventies, Jñanamitra said, 'they doled out hormones like Smarties.' The idea was that if you were serious you would like the effect they had. If changing gender really wasn't right for you, this would quickly make you realise it, and taking hor-mones for a few weeks was reversible and wouldn't do any harm. One of Britain's leading experts in gender reassignment, the consultant psychiatrist Russell Reid, was still prescribing hormones on first appointment until 1997, when the General Medical Council deemed this to be serious professional misconduct.

To want to transition and to go through with it therefore requires real commitment. Many, if not most, people can't imagine why anyone would do it. But then most people have not experienced the power of gender dysphoria: the feeling of being trapped in a body of the wrong gender. No wonder it's hard to imagine: it's almost impossible to even explain. Marland breaks it down into two elements: 'the discomfort within my own body and the discomfort with the social role that had been assigned to me based upon the assumptions people made about my gender. Because it's the sort of thing that is all around us all the time, it's very hard to put a finger on the individual aspects of it.' She recalls a remark by the American academic and film-maker Susan Stryker: 'Gender is the medium through which we swim.' When the gender is wrong, life becomes like swimming through treacle.

However, the relationship between body and identity in gender dysphoria is a paradoxical one. Having the right body is seen as absolutely central to sense of self, but it is possible to have a strong sense of self in the wrong body. Gender dysphoria therefore seems to demonstrate *both* that our bodies are not incidental, but central features of who we are; *and* that our personal identity can be separated from our bodies, if they are the wrong gender.

The paradox is resolved, however, by being more precise. Our sense of self very strongly involves a sense of what body is right for us, but that does not mean we cannot be ourselves in the wrong body. In this sense, a biological man with gender dysphoria is like an engine running on the wrong fuel. A car engine might sound like an unpromising analogy, but bear with me. It is not incidental to an engine that it runs on a particular fuel. A diesel engine won't run on petrol, or vice versa. Some diesel engines, however, will work, just about, on some types of 'wrong' fuel, such as processed vegetable oil. It may splutter and be slow, but it will go. Nevertheless, it remains a diesel engine, not a bioethanol one. In the same way, someone who feels like a woman can live in a man's body, she's just not going to run very smoothly. Having the body of a particular gender is part of her identity, but that identity can survive with a body of another gender.

The transgender experience therefore tells both against those who would make too much of the importance of our bodies for identity and those who would make too little of them. Bodies are hugely important for who we are, because they matter to how we think and experience the world. Identity cannot float free from the physical. But it does not follow that it is in our bodies that we find the pearl of self. Our sense of self is rooted in what we think and how we feel. Our bodies at least in part shape this sense of self, as a plaster cast moulds a statue. But just as no one would confuse the cast with the work of art, so we should not misidentify the body with the core of self.

This is a lesson Jñanamitra perhaps would have learned earlier, had it not been for her Buddhism. Her spiritual and bodily journeys have always intertwined, but not always happily. Jñanamitra doesn't want to give her birth name, but he, as she was, had the typical life of a child whose father was a major in the army. Jñanamitra travelled the world before he was eight and then was sent to boarding school. The gender dysphoria emerged in adolescence, but he blundered on, going to technical college, St Martins Art College and then to the Royal College of Art. 'It wasn't until I was about twenty-five or so that I finally woke up one morning realising that there weren't any magic tricks, there wasn't anything I could do that would sort this,' she says. 'I ended up going on the same day to an introductory meditation class and also my first visit to a self-help group.'

January 1977 was 'one of those wake-up moments', and she went to Charing Cross Hospital, an early pioneering centre of gender reassignment treatment and surgery, and began to transition into Catherine. 'It's a slow process and you end up in a very strange world where the people who know you as male treat you as male and cannot see the emerging woman, and people who see you as a woman treat you as a woman and cannot see the element that's come from being male. It's an extraordinary thing to do with perception, something which actually dogs most transsexuals, so if anybody has known them in their previous gender, they are often very reluctant to reassign them in their minds. You go through a very strange phase where you never quite know how people are going to "read" you, whether they're going to read you as male or female.'

It was therefore a real turning point when Catherine had to go into Accident and Emergency one day and was 'read' as female. 'I did say that I was transsexual and pre-op, but nevertheless they treated me very well and having that affirmation at that point, it took me by surprise, I wasn't expecting it.'

However, when Catherine got more involved with the FWBO again, problems emerged. 'I was very open about being transsexual and I did have some doubts as to whether this was really the way of resolving the issue.' These doubts were fed by the FWBO's founder, Sangharakshita. 'He was so emphatic that physical transformation was not the way to go, and you could deal with this through insight. He frightened me. He really, really frightened me, with some awful karmic consequence of going through the transition.' The Friends of the Western Buddhist Order do not deny the essential genderedness of persons; in fact, quite the opposite, since the sexes are separated for many of its practices. The problem is that it has a rigid view that your gender is determined at birth and that's it.

Jñanamitra knows of others in a similar situation who turned away from the FWBO as a result. But she wanted the Dharma, to follow the path. 'I wanted to join the order so much that I reverted and pursued my ordination process through the male wing of the order. This was extremely difficult for me. I met a great deal of total incomprehension in terms of what I was actually struggling with and working with.'

He, once more, took on the nickname of Kit, 'which is an ambiguous name, it also happens to be the middle syllable of Avalokiteśvara, who's the bodhisattva of compassion.' After eighteen months off the hormones, people were seeing Kit as male again on the street. For twelve years, between 1983 and 1995, Kit followed the ordination process. He worked on his practice, hoping that if he broke through to insight, his gender issues could be resolved. However, 'about three or four years after I was ordained, I began to notice more and more that I'd have a sort of gender dysphoria episode about every month. And I had to finally acknowledge that this was something I hadn't really dealt with at all.'

It all came to a head on a mindfulness retreat. Part of the practice involves observing what thoughts and feelings arise in the mind and considering what such thoughts depend on. What stimulated it? What was the trigger? 'So there I was, mindful of this arising, that arising, and then I realised that underneath all that was an absolutely steady thing, my gender dysphoria, which wasn't arising in dependence upon anything – it was just there. And when I spotted that, I had a most cataclysmic spiritual experience. I've never had anything quite like that since. The whole superstructure of my motivation for pursuing meditation just disappeared like a pack of cards thrown in the wind, and I realised there was absolutely no point struggling and suffering and I might as well go back and see the doctor again. The whole thing that was putting the brakes on was the idea that I could transform this with insight. I did get an insight, but the insight proved that I couldn't transform it with insight.'

She went back into medical treatment without intending to transition but 'the feeling that the true identity was female was so strong and as soon as it was recognised from outside I couldn't stop myself.'

Jñanamitra's story is compelling testimony against those who insist that issues of gender dysphoria can be dealt with without physical change. She tried to do just that, armed with tools of mindful meditation that psychologists who don't necessarily buy into Buddhist metaphysics nevertheless find so powerful that they have adopted them for secular goals. Hers is a limiting case, one that shows how far we can go by trying to separate our identities from our bodies. That she could go so far shows how robust and central the psychological sense of identity is. That this was too far shows how, nonetheless, bodies matter to this sense of identity too.

There is a subtle but vital distinction here, which I alluded to earlier: personal identity cannot float free from the physical, but it is not entirely determined by the physical. To pick up on Susan Stryker's image, our bodies are the media through which we swim. As such they profoundly affect who we are. By analogy, think of how a piece of music is changed if it is played by a symphony orchestra, a rock band or an acoustic folk ensemble. The medium through which it is expressed makes an important difference. Nevertheless, the piece of music itself is not the same as the particular performance by a particular band. Similarly, our lives are like symphonies that last decades, and the instrument we are given to play it on will do a great deal to shape how it sounds. Just as a violin can play notes a bass guitar cannot, and vice versa, so a tall, beautiful, female body provides different possibilities to that of a short, plain male one. To underestimate the extent to which the medium of our existence – the particular body each of us is given – shapes the person we become would be folly. But to think the person just is the medium is equally misguided.

Marland and Jñanamitra are like players who have switched instrument mid-performance. But although this means they have been through far greater changes of identity than most people, this does not seem to give them a radically different sense of the continuities between past and present selves: the song remains the same.

Like other people, they vary in how much they see past selves as continuous with their present ones. Jñanamitra reports having little sense of the various versions of her self being the same person. 'I feel like I've lived several lifetimes these days. It's very weird to look back at my childhood and have a sense of that being me.' It's impossible to say, however, how much of this is to do with her natural dispositions, her gender changes and her Buddhist beliefs, which deny the existence of an enduring self. 'To say "what you truly are" is difficult, because that implies I can look within myself and find something that is "truly are", as it were, whereas what I find is a flux and a flow, something that is continually dependent on conditions, where impulses are arising and falling away.'

Nevertheless, there are some strong continuities. 'I would say I have a recognisable personality style that somebody who knew me before I think would recognise. There are certain interests that persist. I like practical things, I like projects, I like making things, that's always been the case. Those aspects of personality style remain unaltered.' And 'I've always been a female, yes. That has been constant.'

Marland, on the other hand, has the same kind of sense of continuity that many, perhaps most, people have. 'I got lost driving down through Wales a few weeks ago and found myself somewhere I had walked through on several occasions over the last thirty years. Just remembering times past, there are instants I'm holding on to from back then that are so very dear to me. That's still the same me in that sense that I'm still looking out through the same eyes as I was looking out through when I was experiencing that. There's not an old him that I think of in the third person, certainly. I see it as a continuum.'

Gender reassignment is an extreme example, but all selves change over the years. Whether we see them as changes to one self, or as a literal changing of selves, seems to depend more on an individual's perception than on just the extent of the change. Some, it seems, can change bodies yet not change who they really are. Our bodies are not what ultimately give us a sense of the pearl at the heart of self, even if our essential embodiment matters much more than some theorists have believed. This is because we are *bodies of thought*. It is thought – which includes emotions and perceptions, not just rational processes – that makes us who we are, but these thoughts are always embodied. As I said earlier, bodies are essential, but they are not our essences.

Thinking reeds

Transgendered people are not the only ones whose experience cautions against tying sense of self too much or too little to our bodies. There are plenty of other people whose bodies are especially intimately linked to their own sense of who they are. Pianists, athletes, models and gymnasts all require the very particular bodies they have to be the individuals that they have become. Any radical change to their bodies would be a tremendous trauma and would require a total reappraisal of how they should live their lives. But as the philosopher Anthony Quinton rightly says, when such traumas happen, the person does not cease to exist. Core assumptions about what people are and what they do may be shaken or destroyed, but the person who adjusts to this trauma is in critical respects the same person who suffered it. Embodiment is still crucial – they do, after all, still have bodies – but the precise details of the form of it are changeable without out threatening the integrity of the person.

Take the example of model and TV presenter Katie Piper. Her camera-friendly looks were pivotal to the life she had built in television. But on 31 March 2008 a complete stranger, working for her deranged ex-boyfriend, threw sulphuric acid over her face, disfiguring her for life. She was blinded in one eye, and faced years of being fed through a tube and having to wear a transparent face mask twenty-three hours a day.

Talking about the attack eighteen months later, Piper seemed to be endorsing the view that this bodily change resulted in a deep identity change. Looking in the mirror she thought, "'I don't know who that person is." I couldn't identify with them. It was a massive identity crisis.'[4] She had changed. 'I'm never going to be the old Katie. She's like a best friend I once had,' she said. 'She's gone and there's a different one in her place.'[5]

But it also seems to be very clear that this is a case of one person changing, not one person changing into a completely other one. In the most fundamental respects, Piper remains the same woman. She can say things like 'I realise my life before was so superficial' because her life extends before and after the incident. She can report that 'My family have been amazing' because they remained her family, able to recognise and be recognised by her as the same. That indeed was the message viewers were left with at the end of a documentary about her experience. 'I did have these terrible attacks, yeah, I do look totally different physically, but I want to be the woman who got through that and is now living . . . I want to be rid of that and just be Katie.'[6]

An even more extreme bodily transformation happened to the historian Tony Judt. In 2008, he was 'a 61-year-old, very healthy, very fit, very independent, travelling, sports-playing guy'.[7] Eighteen months later, he was a wheelchair-bound quadriplegic, always having to wear a breathing tube through a plastic mask. The motor neuron disorder amyotrophic lateral sclerosis, popularly known as Lou Gehrig's Disease, condemned him to 'progressive imprisonment without parole'.[8] The sentence only ended with his death in August 2010.

'I'm trying to work out what it must mean now to be reduced to the essence of who I am,' he told the journalist Ed Pilkington. 'Pascal's "thinking reed" really does capture it, because I'm just a bunch of dead muscles thinking.' Unable to do anything physical, Judt's very existence had become more and more centred on the mental. Unable to write or take notes, he had to think and remember what he wanted to say, and then dictate it to others. As a result, his memory improved considerably. But 'The pleasures of mental agility are much over-stated, inevitably – as it now appears to me – by those not exclusively dependent upon them. Much the same can be said of well-meaning encouragements to find non-physical compensations for physical inadequacy. That way lies futility. Loss is loss, and nothing is gained by calling it by a nicer name.'[9]

Judt had no time for those who thought that suffering like his was a kind of blessing in disguise. 'This is just hell. Because there is no hope, no help, and you know what the ending is going to be, each day is going to be like the last day only maybe a little bit worse. Sisyphus-like, you are going to have to roll this bloody rock up the hill tomorrow in exactly the same way.'[10] His life became almost intolerable, but it was nonetheless his life. He lost the use of almost all of his body, yet he remained the person trapped in it. Judt demonstrates that although we are tragically dependent on our bodies, our identities are determined by the mental life they enable us to lead. Judt's story is like a philosopher's thought experiment put into sadistic life: what if you were reduced only to your psychological self, with only as much physical support as is minimally required to sustain it? The answer is that your life becomes terrible, but nonetheless it, and you, go on. As Anthony Quinton says, 'characters can survive large and even emotionally disastrous alterations to the physical type of a person's body'.[11]

The idea that our identities are given by our bodies, pure and simple, is too crude. Clearly, what matters most is the inner life of thoughts, feelings and perceptions, which depend on our bodies and are shaped by them, but which are not identical with them. That does, however, suggest that the core of self may yet be physical after all. Perhaps we just haven't been precise enough about what parts of our bodies matter most. No one would think that we are defined by our hearts, lungs or livers, for example, all of which can be transplanted without loss of identity. But isn't there one part of that body that is absolutely essential to who we are? Could our elusive pearl look more like a walnut?

'We have this deep intuition that there is a core, an essence there, and it's hard to shake off, probably impossible to shake off, I suspect. But neuroscience shows that there is no centre in the brain where things do all come together.'

Paul Broks, clinical neuropsychologist

2

Identity on the brain

It's Paris in the springtime, 1982. A four-months-pregnant, 27-year-old American woman, Suzanne Segal, is waiting for a bus. 'In one moment, everything that I had ever taken to be my personal self completely disappeared,' she later recalled. 'It was just gone. As I waited for the bus to approach, something in consciousness was loosening somehow. And when it got there . . . this reference point of an "I", a someone that everything was about and that everything that occurred in life was structured around, was gone. It was like a switch had been turned off. And it was never to turn on again.' She had experienced a blinding, shattering realisation: 'There was no personal self.' Yet 'nothing stopped; the functions continued to function just as before. In fact, better than before. Speaking was still speaking and walking was still walking.'[1]

For ten years, she sought to cure herself of this troubling lack of self, seeing a string of therapists, to no avail. After a while, however, she started to see her transformed state in more spiritual terms. Perhaps what she was feeling was what the Buddha called *anattā*, not-self, the true nature of being? Her lack of sense of self, she came to think, was not a problem, but an insight. She had been gifted the kind of deep spiritual experience that many spent decades of meditation seeking.

Segal wrote a book about her journey, *Collision with the Infinite*, and soon became a star of the international spirituality circuit, a teacher for others to learn from. She taught of 'the Vastness', which sounds very much like the Hindu idea of *brahman*. 'When asked who I am, the only possible answer is: I am the infinite, the Vastness that is the substance of all things. I am no one and everyone, nothing and everything – just as you are.'[2]

In 1996, however, Segal started to experience more regular and powerful 'hits', of the kind that she had first felt stepping onto the Parisian bus. She became exhausted and more withdrawn. Some in her therapy group worried that she had 'lost touch with the Vastness'.[3] At one point she even excitedly phoned a close acquaintance to say that she had discovered she did in fact exist after all, and that 'all the spiritual teachers who taught the non-existence of the abiding self were mistaken'.[4]

It soon became clear that Segal was ill. She had difficulty holding a pen, remembering names and even standing up without feeling dizzy. On 27 February 1997 she went into hospital and had an X-ray, which revealed a massive brain tumour. A week later she had an operation, but the tumour was too large to remove. On 1 April she died, aged forty-two, having spent the last days of her life in a coma.

To many, the manner of Segal's death cast new light on her previous experiences. Brain tumours can grow very slowly indeed, and what seems very likely is that all her 'spiritual' experiences were in fact the result of her cerebral pathology. However, for friends and admirers to accept this would be too much. Imagine believing someone to be a shining spiritual example, only to then conclude that they were in fact simply brain damaged. This would provoke too much 'cognitive dissonance': the mental discomfort caused by holding incompatible beliefs. In such situations humans are very good at eliminating the dissonance by means of rationalisation. And in this case, such a rationalisation is readily available: the tumour was what caused her to *lose* her spiritual insight towards the end; it had nothing to do with her *receiving* it in the first place.

We will never know for sure what the true causal factors were for Segal's experiences, but surely any objective witness would have to conclude that the most likely explanation is neurological. Segal's experience turns out to be not so much that of a collision with the infinite, but a collision of mysticism and philosophy with brain science. Could it be, however, that it is not just in exceptional cases, like Segal's, that science illuminates in a flash what has puzzled sages and philosophers for centuries? Armed with laboratory experiments and fMRI (functional Magnetic Resonance Imaging) scans, can scientists shine a light on the nature of self?

The neurology of I

It would be claiming too much to say that neuroscience has fully explained what selves are and how they can exist. Nevertheless, real progress has been made in recent decades and we are now in a position to at least sketch out how the self is constructed.

The most important finding, which seems to be universally accepted by all researchers into the self and the brain, is that brain research has given up on the search for the pearl of self. As the clinical neuropsychologist Paul Broks put it to me, 'We have this deep intuition that there is a core, an essence there, and it's hard to shake off, probably impossible to shake off, I suspect. But it's true that neuroscience shows that there is no centre in the brain where things do all come together.' The unity of the self is not to be explained in terms of a single, unified brain region, which acts as the master controller.

This is not what common sense would expect, but philosophers have anticipated it. For some time now, they have been wary of explanations which commit what is known as the homunculus fallacy.

This is best explained through the example of vision. Armed with an elementary knowledge of how the eye works, it is tempting to think that light shines on the retina and then the brain creates from this a single, three-dimensional image. But who sees this image? The temptation is to think (or perhaps more usually assume) that there is a kind of mind's eye which inspects the image in the brain. But then how does this 'mind's eye' see this image? It cannot be that there is a little person – a homunculus – in our brains which watches mental images. If that were the case, we'd have to ask what was going on inside the head of that homunculus. Would there be another mental image, and if so, what would be seeing that? An even smaller homunculus? If we continued to explain each stage in the same way, we'd end up with an infinite number of ever smaller homunculi, each packed Russian-doll-like into our brains. Such an infinite regress could never explain how any seeing actually went on at all.

What is true of vision is true of the mental in general. Daniel Dennett uses the term 'Cartesian theater' to label this misguided way of thinking. The idea here is that it is easily assumed that in order to explain consciousness, we have to think of there being a single, unified centre of consciousness somewhere 'inside' us, whether we think this is an immaterial soul or a special part of the physical brain. But this cannot explain the unity of consciousness at all. You cannot *explain* the unity of experience by simply positing an inner, unified experiencer. That simply begs the question: how is unity of experience possible in the first place?

So even before neuroscience shone a light on how experience is unified in the brain, philosophers had a theoretical reason to think that, whatever the answer was, it couldn't be that there was a kind of 'inner self' doing the work. Neuroscience has in effect discovered through experiment and observation what philosophers had concluded just by thinking.

So how does it all come together? It's too soon to say that there is a definitive answer, but there are sufficient similarities between different researchers' views to suggest that the outlines of an answer are in place. The central insight is that the sense of self is constructed from a variety of different brain systems working together. Some of these are very old and are shared with very unsophisticated animals. Others are unique to higher mammals.

A now standard model for categorising these different functions is known as the triune brain, and was proposed by Paul D. MacLean.[5] This model divides the brain up into three broad regions, which correspond both to the actual physiology of the brain now and also to their evolutionary age. The oldest of these is often called our 'reptilian brains' or the R-complex, which comprises the brain stem and cerebellum. This regulates basic, automatic functions such as breathing and instinctive behaviour. It first evolved during the Triassic period, more than 200 million years ago.

Not quite so old is the limbic system, or the paleomammalian brain, which emerged during the Jurassic period, 206–144 million years ago. This regulates emotional reactions, including fight or flight responses, sexual desire and feeding. Anatomically, it comprises the amygdala, the hypothalamus and the hippocampus.

The newest and most advanced parts of our brains are a mere 24–55 million years old, born during the Eocene and Oligocene epochs. This is the neomammalian brain, otherwise known as the neocortex or cerebral cortex. Higher brain functions like logical reasoning and episodic memory depend on it. Only mammals have a neocortex, and it is most developed in primates, especially humans.

Of course, this is just a model, and it should not be thought that the neocortex and limbic system are layered on top of the reptilian brain like some kind of neural lasagne. In reality, the systems evolved gradually and are deeply interconnected. Nevertheless, there are clear enough differences in both the age and functioning of each of the three parts of the brain for it to be useful for us to think of them as three distinct areas.

Almost all researchers into the way the brain creates a sense of self give accounts of how all these brain areas make their contributions and work together. So although, for instance, the neocortex is critical, it would be wrong to conclude that the self is located in it. That is because the brain's higher functions depend on lower ones.

Todd Feinberg, a professor of neurology and psychology, offers one of the most developed theories about how the different brain regions work together to create a sense of self. The key concept he utilises is that of a *nested hierarchy*. Hierarchical systems come in two varieties. 'A non-nested hierarchy,' writes Feinberg, 'has a pyramidal structure with a clear-cut top and bottom in which higher levels control the operation of lower levels.'[6] Feinberg's favourite example is of an army. Each level of the hierarchy is independent, and all control comes from the top. Feinberg argues that this is not how the self works, and the fact that there is no central command spot in the brain suggests he's right.

However, there is another kind of hierarchy: one which is nested. Nested hierarchies can be visualised as concentric circles, with the smallest circle in the centre at the 'bottom' of the hierarchy and the largest, outer circle at the 'top' of it. To say such a hierarchy is nested is simply to say that the top levels incorporate the lower ones. Higher levels are not therefore independent of lower ones. Take away the lowest level and the highest is left with a donut-like hole at its centre, and it just can't function.

All living things, says Feinberg, are nested hierarchies. 'At the lower levels of an organism are organelles that are combined to produce single cells that are in turn organised to produce tissues, which are then combined to produce organs that are ultimately organised to produce an entire living organism.'[7] You may not understand the precise biological terms here (I don't) but the principle is clear:

'lower' or 'smaller' elements are not separate from the larger, higher ones. Rather, they constitute those higher parts and are incorporated into them. So, unlike in a non-nested hierarchy, each level cannot be physically separated. Even more importantly, control does not come from the top down. Rather, the whole system puts constraints on what it can and can't do and there is no single centre of control.

MacLean's triune brain is a hierarchical model, but is it nested? Physically speaking, Feinberg says, it is not, because the higher-level regions, such as the thalamus, are not composed of the lower-level regions. However, *functionally*, the self is indeed a nested hierarchy. This is because the higher functions of self, such as self-consciousness, are not independent of lower functions, such as basic awareness of environment, but incorporate and depend on them.

To see how this applies more concretely in the case of first-person experience, take the broadest distinction between higher and lower functions of the self. Different theorists use different descriptions, but most distinguish between what is variously called a 'minimal', 'core' or 'implicit' self and the 'extended' or 'autobiographical' self.[8]

The minimal self is the most primitive kind of self-awareness. Any creature which is able to in some sense distinguish itself from the environment and other things has a minimal self. The reptilian brain has sufficient resources to enable this. However, to say that even lizards have selves is highly misleading, because this kind of awareness is almost certainly entirely in the moment. The lizard has some sense of itself *at a time* but not *over time*.

Human beings, perhaps uniquely, have autobiographical selves. We have a sense of our distinct existence which extends to the past and the future. This is usually highly developed. The narratives we have of our pasts, for instance, are rich in detail. Clearly, the development of episodic memory is essential to the development of the autobiographical self. In contrast, most, if not all, animal memory is simply a form of learned response. Your dog remembers you in that it recognises you as its pack leader, but it is very unlikely that it fondly recalls past walks, as you do. That difference is a core part of what enables you to develop the autobiographical self which is either absent or very limited in the dog.

As well as hindsight, foresight is a characteristic part of autobiographical selves. We can plan ahead with incomparably more sophistication than even the most cognitively advanced primates. Chimpanzees can at best anticipate only a few steps ahead; human beings can make plans for entire cities that span years.

Between the minimal core self and the fully developed autobiographical self is a continuum, of course. Different theorists carve up this space in different ways, and attribute different levels of importance to different brain regions. But all would agree that the core self is nested, in Feinberg's sense, in the autobiographical self. You don't need to know a lot of neuroscience to see that this must be true: in order to have a sense of oneself over time, one first needs to have a basic sense of oneself as different from other creatures and the environment. Studies of the brain show *how* this is so, but that it *must* be so is a conceptual necessity.

It would be misleading to suggest that neuroscientists speak with one voice on the self, but all the leading people in the field do seem to agree on a few key fundamentals: that higher functions of self build on and incorporate lower ones; that there is no part of the brain at which it all comes together; that there is a continuum between the human sense of self and that of the lizard, and that there is no sharp dividing line between creatures with autobiographical selves and those without.

But does this have any deep philosophical implications? Can it, and should it, change how we think about ourselves?

A robust fragility

The clinical neuropyschologist Paul Broks has a taste for the philosophical, so he is a good man to discuss these issues with. 'I've always been interested in the big woolly questions,' he told me when I went to meet him at his office at the University of Plymouth. Broks's first degree was in fact in philosophy, 'but I had this terrible streak of pragmatism when I realised it was very hard to make a living in that kind of line unless you're very brilliant, or very dull actually. You can spend a lifetime writing theses on "if" and "then", and if you want to do that, then that's fine.'

When his career took him to clinical psychology, specialising in neuropsychology, 'all those old questions then came back again, because a lot of what goes on in clinical practice has to do with those big questions: is it the same person post brain surgery, post stroke, post amnesia?' Broks has written eloquently about these issues, first in magazines and newspapers, and then in his book *Into the Silent Land*. His prose evokes the strangeness, mysteries and paradoxes of our experiences of self, usually starting from pathological cases, but using them to shine peculiar light on our ordinary experience.

These strange case studies reveal another riddle of the self: that it is at the same time frighteningly fragile and astonishingly robust. Its fragility is shown in the numerous cases where the many elements of the self which normally go together can come apart, completely transforming how the individual relates to her self, the world or both.

Consider, for example, Cotard Syndrome, which Broks describes as 'a kind of nihilistic delusion that parts of the body don't exist and that in extreme cases the whole of the body doesn't exist and they believe that they're dead'. People with Cotard Syndrome 'don't believe they exist, they have no sense of being alive in the moment, but they'll give you their life history. So there's the autobiographical bit and there's a story that they weave together, so there is a sense of self there, but it's a sense of self which is discontinued, or defunct.'

Another example is found in people suffering from temporal lobe epilepsy, in an experience called transient epileptic amnesia. 'People will tell you that it's so weird,' explains Broks. 'The world around them stays just as real and vivid – in fact, even more vivid sometimes – but they have no sense of who they are. It might be minutes, maybe ten minutes, maybe half an hour. They lose all sense of who they are, what their immediate goals are, usually where they are. The environment seems real but unfamiliar, but they know *that they are*. What is it that Descartes said? I know that I am, but what is this I that I know?' This sounds very similar to Suzanne Segal's far longer-term experience, and to the kind of state of selflessness that many spiritual seekers aspire to. Isn't it strange, however, that the very same state which people aspire to achieve through spiritual discipline can be created by what, under the lens of neuropsychology, is a freak pathology?

'When that book was published, I had a lot of correspondence from Buddhists and Zen meditators who said, well clearly you're a Buddhist because there are so many Buddhist ideas in there,' but, no, he wasn't. Indeed, he finds it 'a strange notion that you might spend years on top of a mountain trying to achieve that kind of state'.

The literature on neural pathology is stuffed full of cases where the normally integrated self in some sense falls apart. The most striking, and probably most discussed, experiment involves the 'split-brain' patients of Roger Sperry and Michael Gazzaniga. As a last-resort experimental procedure to treat severe epilepsy, surgeons severed the corpus callosum, which connects the two hemispheres of the brain. The results of this operation – called a commissurotomy – was that the epilepsy was indeed much reduced. But Sperry and Gazzaniga conducted some experiments which revealed a remarkable, unforeseen side effect.

Patients were asked to focus on a dot in the centre of a screen. Words and images were then flashed up for a few seconds on either the right or left side of the screen. When these appeared on the right side of the screen, the patients were easily able to say what they were. But when they appeared on the left of the screen, they claimed to have seen nothing. However, it seemed that in some ways, they had indeed seen something. If asked, for instance, to draw an object with their left hand, they would draw what had just been shown on the screen, all the time denying they had seen any such thing. They could also manipulate or use the object normally with their left hands. So what was going on?

The way in which vision works is that information from the right visual field is processed by the left-brain hemisphere, while information from the left visual field is processed by the right hemisphere. But it is the left hemisphere which (in most people) controls speech. Because normally the corpus callosum allows the two hemispheres to communicate, this presents no practical difficulty for most people. But the corpus callosum had been severed in Sperry and Gazzaniga's patients, so this information exchange could not occur. That meant that if you controlled carefully which hemisphere received information from the environment, you could effectively make one hemisphere aware of something that the other was not. What is astonishing about this is that for this to be possible, there would have to be *two* centres of awareness in the individual concerned. But isn't the very definition of a self that of a single, unified subject of awareness? Commissurotomy therefore seems to show that selves can be divided – at least temporarily – or that they needn't have just one centre of consciousness after all.

The self is fragile in countless other ways. Clinical case studies have been piling up ever since the first and most famous, that of the Vermont railroad worker Phineas Gage. One morning in September 1848 Gage was setting down gunpowder to blast rocks. He didn't do a good job: he accidentally detonated the blast early, sending a 13½-lb iron rod, three feet seven inches long and 1¼ inches wide, straight through his eye socket, through parts of his frontal lobe and out of the top of his skull. But not only did Gage survive, he was only unconscious for a quarter of an hour, spoke coherently and clearly after that, and was pain-free the next day.

But something had changed. Gage had been hard-working, polite, affable and widely respected. After the accident he became obstinate, rude, capricious and impatient. Friends said he was 'no longer' Gage. What was thought to be his real self, his core personality which defined who he was, had been transformed by a single bolt.

Writers like Oliver Sacks, Paul Broks and Todd Feinberg have vividly described numerous other strange cases, often with detailed neurological explanations. Reading them, one is struck by the fragility of what we take to be permanent, essential features of our selves. 'The very first clinical placement I did was at the Rivermead rehab hospital in Oxford,' says Broks, 'and that was a profound experience because you saw people who had been involved in road traffic accidents through no fault of their own and you realise how fragile the sense of self is, how fragile the mind is.'

But this fragility is only one half of the story. Despite these enormous upheavals, 'sense of self is generally pretty robust,' says Broks. The split selves of the commissurotomy patients, for instance, only emerge in specific experimental conditions. In real life, they find ways of retaining a unified experience of the world. Even with a split brain, we are able to function as though we had a unified mind. As Feinberg puts it, 'The fact that one hemisphere may oppose the other in the split brain only highlights the extraordinary fact that under most circumstances these patients behave in a fully integrated fashion and subjectively feel unified.' Nor is this resilience of the unified sense of self unique to commissurotomy patients. 'I have encountered patients with other neurological conditions who demonstrate a remarkable resiliency of the self despite their neurological damage,' says Feinberg.[9] If the unified self is an illusion, it is a very persistent one.

This resilience can extend to how we see others too. Consider, for example, a story Broks told me. 'This guy had a severe head injury, so severe that he didn't even recognise his four-year-old son. I did a home visit and this little boy came into the room and he picks him up and gives him a big hug and introduces me, but it wasn't his son, it was his next-door neighbour's son. He changed temperamentally. He would fly off into these most awful tantrums, which he did when I was with him. And I talked to his wife afterwards and asked, "How do you cope with this, how do you deal with this?" because it happened quite a lot. And she said, "Well when it happens I tell myself it's not really Geoff. When he does that he's not Geoff any more." But if it's not Geoff why does she stay with him? What's the commitment? What's it based on? It's that belief that at some level it *really is* Geoff. But that's a magical belief ultimately, isn't it? It's a magical belief that there's some essential Geoffness about Geoff. But if you pick away at it, there isn't really, it falls apart.'

In the living of normal life, however, it will always come back together again. Broks says that, despite his intellectual convictions, he lives as a 'soul theorist' or 'ego theorist' who persists with the belief in a fixed core of self. 'I think we probably all do, because that's the way we've evolved biologically and sociologically to think and behave. Neuroscience is chipping and will chip away at the cherished ideas that go with that, like the idea that we're autonomous agents with free will and moral choice. But it won't stop us living by them and it probably shouldn't.'

No matter how tenuous a notion the self seems to be under scientific scrutiny, we cannot abandon it because it is the thread on which we hang our lives. 'Very rarely do you find people saying I'm not the same person as I was. We all tend to think there's a connection between the four-year-old child on our first day at school and us now.'

However, if you try to identify wherein that sameness lies, you find very little. 'Physically we're not the same, psychologically we're not the same, genetically we're the same but that doesn't mean anything really; we may have certain patterns of brain organisation that predispose us temperamentally in certain ways, so we're the same in that sense but then lots of other people probably have the same organisational patterns, so every which way you look at it we're not really the same. What makes us the same is that we *believe* we're the same.'

Sense of self over time is therefore 'the story that we tell ourselves that keeps us together.' We may go through major transformations, not just brain injuries, but what psychologists call 'emotional insult', such as the break-up of relationships or a bereavement. 'Are we the same people when we come through them? In some sense yes, in some sense no, but it seems we have no choice but to believe that we are.' Belief in the enduring self is therefore, Broks believes, a kind of magical thinking. But that is not to disparage it: the magic has real power, 'it's what we're built on'.

It seems to me, however, that the robustness of the self must rest on more than just wishful thinking. Or at least, such wishful thinking can only work if there is an underlying mechanism that makes it believable. So what could explain the strange combination of fragility and robustness that characterises the self?

The answer is perhaps that the fragility is the strength. A pearl may be hard and distinct, but smash it and it's utterly destroyed. A composite or amalgam, on the other hand, is of its nature a collection of things. That means items can come and go, or be damaged, without necessarily terminally destroying the character of the whole. Could this explain why we have a strong sense of self, in the absence of any pearl at the heart of it? Could it be that the self is not a single thing, but a kind of composite? It's a possibility we'll return to, but certainly brain science suggests something like this must be true.

Michael Gazzaniga explains one aspect of this when he discusses why it is that a split-brain patient 'does not find one side of the brain missing the other'. His simple answer is that 'we don't miss what we no longer have access to'. Consciousness of self emerges from a network of thousands or millions of conscious moments. This means that when we lose bits, the way a split-brain patient does, we don't sense anything as lost at all. Gazzaniga explains this thought with the metaphor of a pipe organ. 'The thousands or millions of conscious moments that we each have reflect one of our networks being "up for duty". These networks are all over the place, not in one specific location. When one finishes, the next one pops up. The pipe-organ-like device plays its tune all day long. What makes emergent human consciousness so vibrant is that our pipe organ has lots of tunes to play.'[10]

Neuroscientist Antonio Damasio also has something to contribute to the resolution of the riddle. Damasio believes that his view 'resolves the apparent paradox identified by William James – that the self in our stream of consciousness changes continuously as it moves forward in time, even as we retain a sense that the self remains the same while our existence continues'. His solution is that 'the seemingly changing self and the seemingly permanent self, although closely related, are not one entity but two'.[11] That is to say, what seems permanent is the autobiographical self, and what seems to be changing is the core self. Whether or not Damasio has this exactly right, his broad approach does seem to be correct. The unity and permanence we feel over time largely depends on our ability to construct an autobiographical narrative that links our experiences over time. But individual experiences and sense of self at any particular time can vary enormously. What is more, the autobiographical self is very good at self-revision. In effect, we are constantly rewriting our histories to keep our inner autobiographies coherent.

The fragility and robustness of the self is therefore no paradox, but another riddle that makes perfect sense when you understand enough about it. In short, the robustness of the self lies in the fact that it is not a thing at all, but a product of the complex interaction of parts of the brain and body. If something has no essence, then it is hard to destroy it by removing any given part. This means that very few, if any, parts are critical to its existence, and so it can adapt to sometimes massive losses. However, self does still depend on that functioning brain, and the wrong kind of malfunction can dramatically change it or completely destroy it.

To put it another way, the self is a construction of the mind, one flexible enough to withstand constant renovation, partial demolition and reconstruction, but one that can be brought down if the foundations are undermined. The idea of the self as a construction is one that many want to resist, because it seems to imply that it is not real. But of course constructions can be perfectly real. It is important to distinguish between 'mere constructs', which exist solely as ideas, and real constructions, which we pick up, use and live in. The 'average American family' is a mere construct, but the house at 127 Acacia Avenue is a real construction.

However, although neuroscience and psychology may both challenge and clarify our ideas of the self, it is not clear that they can in any way have the last word on them. 'I don't think that the self is ultimately a scientifically tractable question,' says Broks. 'That notion of the unified, continuous, singular self is challenged at various points, I think, but that doesn't mean we suddenly abandon the idea of the unified, continuous, singular self.'

The limits of what neuroscience can contribute to our understanding of self was made evident to me as I read more and more about how the brain constructs a sense of self. The findings I have reported here do seem to illuminate the issue, or at least shine a light different from the torch of philosophers, one which brings out certain details more clearly. But if you go into details, the real nuts and bolts, you rarely, if ever, come across anything that takes us forward philosophically. All you get is more detail about the precise mechanisms by which self emerges from brains. While this is extremely important work, it adds little or nothing to the question that faces each of us as individuals, namely, what are we? It's like a car. In order to drive and maintain it, you have to know how it works. But you don't need to know the details of the chemical reactions that make the internal combustion engine possible, or the fundamental physics which explains the gravity that keeps the wheels on the road. Likewise, a basic knowledge of the mechanics of mind is very useful knowledge for the user, but probing the inner workings of synapses is a specialist endeavour that we can happily leave to others.

There are, however, two highly significant features of the self that scientific knowledge pulls into focus. Firstly it underlines very strongly the fact that there is no pearl at the heart of self. The apparent unity of self is the result of a highly organised play of parts. The second is that central to the ordinary sense of self is the construction of what has been called here the autobiographical self, and this depends, more than anything else, on memory. Could it be, then, that there is indeed a kind of pearl of self, one that is not a thing, but a store of memories?

'Just remembering times past, there are instants I'm holding on to from back then that are so very dear to me. That's still the same me in that sense that I'm still looking out through the same eyes.'

Drusilla Marland, who has lived as a man and as a woman

3

Memory makers

R obert stands holding his wife Linda's hand. The white-bearded 65-year-old smiles and talks to her with the ease that you'd expect after forty-two years of marriage. Linda, however, does not, cannot, reciprocate. Nothing in her behaviour suggests she even recognises him, and all that comes from her mouth is a constant stream of noise, made up of the same, indistinct, single-syllable sound, a kind of mix of shushing and chattering.

Robert turns and talks to me, still holding Linda's hand, as though she weren't there. He describes her condition and progress with absolutely no sense at all that she might be listening or understanding. If there is contradiction in his behaviour it is only because there is a contradiction in Linda, and his relationship to her. He is both with her and not with her; she is there and not there; they are both together and apart.

Linda is in the late stages of dementia. She was relatively young when she fell ill with it, and the disease's progression has been swift. Robert shows me a photograph from eighteen months before, at a Christmas party. You can see that she was still lucid then. She could share a meal, laugh with friends and family whom she fully recognised. Now, there is at most an occasional small response that suggests Robert is not just anyone.

Kathleen Wilkes complained that the philosophy of personal identity depends far too much on fanciful thought experiments, and that this is entirely unnecessary, because real life provides all the test cases we need.[1] Dementia is perhaps the cruellest and most revealing example. Many philosophers have argued that we are constituted by a psychologically continuous web of thoughts, feelings, beliefs and memories. Dementia says, well, okay, let's pick that web apart, piece by piece and see if anything of you remains.

A brief history of memory

Dementia comes in several forms and can impair a large number of cognitive functions, but the most important and most noticeable of these is memory. Before looking at what dementia tells us about why and to what extent memory matters for identity, it is worth spending some time looking at what it has historically been taken to be, and how we now understand memory actually working.

The idea that memory is vital for identity is a common one, perhaps most simply and powerfully expressed by Leibniz in 1686. 'Suppose that someone could suddenly become King of China,' he asked, 'but only on condition of forgetting what he had been, as if he had just been born all over again. Would it not in practice, or in terms of perceivable effects, be the same as if he had been annihilated, and a King of China had been created at the same instant in his place? And that is something which that individual could have no reason to want.'[2]

Similar thoughts informed one of the first modern advocates of psychological continuity as the key to personal identity, the seventeenth-century philosopher John Locke. Such was the emphasis he placed on memory that he has been widely attributed with holding a 'memory criterion' of personal identity.

Locke defined 'person' in psychological terms, as a 'thinking intelligent being that has reflection and can consider itself as itself, the same thinking thing in different times and places'. The key to personal identity is therefore consciousness: 'For since consciousness always accompanies thinking, and 'tis that, that makes every one to be, what he calls self; and thereby distinguishes himself from all other thinking things, in this alone consists personal Identity, i.e. the sameness of a rational Being: And as far as this consciousness can be extended backwards to any past Action or Thought, so far reaches the Identity of that Person.'[3]

This has widely been interpreted to mean, as two recent commentators put it, that 'a person at two different times will have the same consciousness and hence will be the same person [if] the person at a later time remembers having experienced and done what the person at the earlier time experienced and did'.[4] This would mean, incidentally, that almost no one is the same as their infant selves, since most people have no autobiographical recall at all of the first three or four years of life.[5]

As a matter of fact, Locke almost certainly did not have a conception of personal identity that rested entirely on continuity of memory. That is just as well, for it is evident that this would be far too simplistic. A clear, decisive objection was made against such a view by Thomas Reid:

Suppose a brave officer to have been flogged when a boy at school for robbing an orchard, to have taken a standard from the enemy in his first campaign, and to have been made a general in advanced life; suppose, also, which must be admitted to be possible, that, when he took the standard, he was conscious of his having been flogged at school, and that, when made a general, he was conscious of his taking the standard, but had absolutely lost the consciousness of his flogging.

These things being supposed, it follows, from Mr Locke's

doctrine, that he who was flogged at school is the same person who took the standard, and that he who took the standard is the same person who was made a general. Whence it follows, if there be any truth in logic, that the general is the same person with him who was flogged at school. But the general's consciousness does not reach so far back as his flogging; therefore, according to Mr Locke's doctrine, he is not the person who was flogged. Therefore the general is, and at the same time is not, the same person with him who was flogged at school.[6]

Although Reid's objection hits the bullseye, in an important respect both he and Locke are looking at the wrong target. Both philosophers make simplistic assumptions that do not match up to what we know about how memory actually works. The model they use links events and memories in a very straightforward way, as though memory creates a record of an event and keeps it filed until such time as it is lost. We now know that memory works very differently. Each time a memory is recalled, it is changed in some way. Memories are not passive chunks of information. Rather, memory is an active process, the contents of which are forever in flux. Any memories that the general had, of raising the standard or of being flogged, would be a mixture of accurate recollections, distortions of time, confabulation and mistakes made concrete by repeated recall.

So when we talk about 'consciousness reaching back', we must not imagine that it does so by stretching directly over the intervening years. Consciousness does not so much 'reach back' as link to the past by what a contemporary heir of Locke, Derek Parfit, calls 'overlapping chains' of psychological connectedness. Even this image is somewhat misleading, as 'chains' suggests sturdier links than the far more fluid ones of real memory.

Thought of in this way, Reid's example can be reinterpreted as showing how we are psychologically connected with past selves by memory, even in the absence of a specific memory of a particular past self. The old general may not remember stealing the apple, but he remembers raising the standard, and the person who raised the standard remembered stealing the apple. None of these memories are in the form of direct connection with the younger self: all memories are mediated by recall and forgetfulness. Nonetheless, there are chains of connection between the general and the officer, and the officer and the boy, so even though there is no conscious memory connection between the general and the boy, there is continuity of memory between them.

This continuity, however, is much more precarious than we would like to believe. Memory is extremely unreliable. In one now famous experiment, the psychologist Elizabeth Loftus was able to make up to a third of experiment subjects believe that they had met Bugs Bunny at Disneyland just by showing them a fake advert of a child hugging the rabbit at the theme park with the headline 'Remember the magic?' Such a memory had to be false, because Bugs Bunny is a Warner Brothers, not a Disney, character.[7] Experiments like this show that the brain is not like a tape recorder. 'Memories don't just fade, as the old saying would have us believe; they also grow,' wrote Loftus et al. 'Every time we recall an event, we must reconstruct the memory, and with every recollection the memory may be changed . . . Truth and reality, when seen through the filter of our memories, are not objective facts but subjective, interpretive realities.'[8]

The relationship between memory and sense of self is therefore a rather complicated one. It is often said that we construct our sense of self from our memories, but in some ways we construct our memories from our sense of self. This dynamic is dramatised in Christopher Nolan's film *Memento*. The lead character, Leonard, has lost the ability to lay down new memories. His working memory is only a couple of minutes. To cope with this, he has devised a system of making notes – the most important tattooed on his body – to remind him of the key things he must remember to avenge the murder of his wife.

Without giving too much away, by the end of the film it becomes obvious that Leonard's note-taking involves not just the recording of important facts, but the systematic erasure of uncomfortable ones. And although his amnesia is unusual, it does indeed reflect something important about how we use memory to construct the image of ourselves and our lives that fits with what we want. We all ignore and do not commit to memory facts and events that conflict with the way we see ourselves and the world. We remember selectively, usually without conscious effort or desire to do so. And yet because we believe memory records facts, objectively, we fail to see that all this means that we are constructing ourselves and the world.

Memories are therefore rather complicated building blocks of the self. For that reason, there is no simple memory criterion of personal identity that passes muster. What's more, modern advocates of psychological continuity as the basis for personal identity over time see memory as just one of a number of psychological connections over time that contribute to this continuity, and they see this continuity in terms of overlapping connections, not rigid, constant ties to each stage of our past selves. These connections include temperament, desire, intention and belief. A person who had a good memory but woke up each day with a different personality or set of preferences would not experience enough psychological continuity to provide unity for the self.

Nevertheless, for all its fallibility and constructed nature, it is clear that memory is one of the most, if not *the* most, important of these connections. Psychologists and neuroscientists are perhaps more explicit about this than philosophers. As we have seen, the autobiographical self, on which many claim the sense of identity depends, is constructed largely on the foundations of memory. If this is true, we should expect any radical disruption of memory to diminish, if not entirely destroy, the identity of the individual. Real life, tragically, provides plenty of examples that test this claim.

Goldfish living

In the late summer of 1953, in an operating theatre in Hartford Hospital, Connecticut, a neurosurgeon called William B. Scoville drilled into the head of a patient known as H.M. and sucked out a fistful of his brain. To use more clinical language, he removed parts of H.M.'s medial temporal lobes and some surrounding tissue, meaning the patient lost most of the hippocampus, the para-hippocampal gyrus, the entorhinal and perirhinal cortex and the amygdala.

Such extreme measures were thought necessary because H.M. suffered particularly frequent and intense epileptic fits. The operation was successful, in the sense that H.M. was indeed cured of this curse. But the improvements came at a terrible price: H.M. lost the ability to lay down any new memories. He remembered nothing that happened in the remaining fifty-five years of his life.

H.M.'s memory would often be compared to that of a goldfish, and his life certainly ended up being lived in something of a goldfish bowl. His became one of the most celebrated case studies in neuropathology. The most extensive work with H.M. was done by Dr Brenda Milner. 'He was a very gracious man, very patient, always willing to try these tasks I would give him,' she once said. 'And yet every time I walked in the room, it was like we'd never met.'

H.M.'s loss was an immeasurable gain to the science of memory. Experiments conducted by Milner showed that although H.M. formed no new memories, he could learn new tasks. This showed that episodic memory – recollection of facts and events – worked quite differently from procedural memory – ability to remember how to do things. It also shed light on the different brain mechanisms underlying short- and long-term memory, since H.M. could hold information for about twenty seconds in 'working memory' quite normally. It also helped develop the distinction between explicit and implicit memory: memories we are aware of and those that affect our thought and behaviour without any conscious recollection.

But perhaps most interesting of all is what H.M.'s loss suggests about the importance of memory for identity. 'Say it however you want,' the President of America's Society for Neuroscience Thomas Carew said when H.M. died in December 2008, 'what H.M. lost, we now know, was a critical part of his identity.'[9] Few would disagree with that. The question is what, if anything, of his identity remained?

What seems clear is that H.M. did retain some sense of self. This is certainly the view Philip J. Hilts formed, having spent a long time with H.M. while writing his book *Memory's Ghost*. This residual sense of self was a 'sharply realistic' idea of the kind of person H.M. was. 'The memory of our own traits does not depend on our collection of personal memories,' writes Hilts. 'They inhabit separate provinces. We do not arrive at summaries about ourselves by concluding from instances.'[10]

However, to say that H.M.'s amnesia left his self intact is to go too far. A person is not just a relatively stable collection of dispositions and character traits. It is for good reason that theorists of the self always consider the unity of the individual *over time* as well as *at a time*. To be a person is to live a life with a past, present and future. H.M. had a past, but it ran adrift from his present in 1953. Although he had some retrograde amnesia, he always remembered most of his life prior to his operation. But memories only bind the self sufficiently if they are part of an ongoing narrative that comes up to date. H.M.'s past was out of sync with his present. When he saw photographs of himself with his mother, taken years after his operation, he recognised his mother but not himself. In his mind, he was always twenty-seven.

Interestingly, however, it does seem that tacit memory enabled him to learn that he had in fact aged, even though he held no explicit belief that he had done so. So when asked if he had grey hair he said he did not know, but he showed no surprise when he saw himself in the mirror, suggesting he had got used to the way he looked. When asked his age and what year it was, he initially always answered 'twenty-seven' and '1953' but eventually offered wildly different guesses.

The case of H.M. therefore fits the claim that memory is the most significant connection we have with our past selves, and its rupture causes real damage to the self. But memory is not the only connection. If there is a continuity of key character traits, there will be some, albeit a radically diminished, continuity of the self too. 'A man does not consist of memory alone,' wrote the psychologist A.R. Luria, 'he has feeling, will, sensibilities, moral feeling – matters of which neuropsychology cannot speak.'[11] That is why H.M. remained recognisably H.M., even though he had lost a huge part of who he was.

Dementia

What is true of H.M. seems also to be true of people with dementia. The loss of memory is a severe attack on the self, but it does not entirely defeat it. It is a matter of interpretation whether you think what remains is not much more than a residue of the person or something of their essential core. This is why people who have seen dementia close up differ considerably in how they think about the person the sufferer has become, and why the same people may hold paradoxical views about the sufferers.

On the one hand, many will talk about relatives and loved ones in advanced stages of dementia as 'no longer there'. One woman, Rachel, told me that by the time her mother died she had already 'gone' and was 'just like a zombie'. She visited her a few times a year but really wasn't sure why, since there was no recognition or response. Echoing what many relatives of dementia sufferers think, she told me, 'People asked me at the funeral if I was sad, and I said no, because I had lost her years ago.'

This response is clearly congruent with views of the self that place our inner lives, not our bodies or brains, at the heart of our identity. The person is viewed not as the particular human animal, but the psychologically continuous person embodied in it, and when that continuity is destroyed by dementia, the person is seen as having been destroyed too. Of course, the self on this view does not die in an instant. Rather, in an analogy several people I spoke to endorsed, it is more like a dimmer switch being gradually turned down on the self. But does the light actually go out before the body packs up? There must surely be some individual variation here, both in the sufferer and in the relative's ability to see in the dark, or perhaps imagine what they can see. Another relative of a sufferer, Boris, thought that there was always some residue of his mother's self dimly present, right to the end, particularly in terms of her bolshy, argumentative nature. There's an echo of H.M. here: for some, it seems that the persistence of a set of personality traits is itself sufficient to say that something of the self persists too. Boris, however, also had the self-awareness to question whether or not the love he felt was really for what remained of his mother, or was testimony to what he remembered of her from before.

Yet this view of dementia as the dimmer switch of the soul is not universally shared. Another relative, Jill, offered a very different metaphor: dementia was like an infra-red lamp that revealed what was always there, but was usually missed in the bright light of ordinary life. Dementia took the lid off darker aspects of her mother's personality. The balance was shifted within her existing personality; she did not acquire a completely new one. The evil looks and snide remarks were simply no longer repressed. Although her memory went, along with her ability to recognise her daughter, in Jill's view she was very much 'still there'. Jill had no sense of a reduction or diminution of the self.

This is closer to the view taken by Janet and her daughter Jackie, who run the care home where Linda is now a resident. Janet utterly rejects the common view that dementia is the slow death of the self. 'I have a belief that dementia actually makes you more like yourself, so rather than rob you of your self, it robs you of all the exterior things that you pile on through life, all the baggage that you carry and the layers. What you're left with at the end of the day with dementia is the core person, the soul, or whatever term you want to put on it. We've described it as an onion. If you peel an onion, from the brown skin outwards, you've got lots and lots of layers. When you get right to the centre of the onion you get to a little pearl in the middle and you can't peel any more off it. It seems to me that it's the real essence of the person.'

What gives this view some credence is the extent to which personality remains, even as memory and other cognitive capacities fail. 'One of the things with the residents here that you see time and time again is that they behave in character,' says Jackie. 'So if they've been aggressive, nasty people all their lives, then that's how they respond to any stimuli here. If they use humour to get through things, they're the ones who are singing and dancing to get through things here. The idea of people being aggressive and it being the dementia that's causing that – well the dementia doesn't cause the aggression. People who might not have shown how angry they were in the past are more disinhibited, so if they're irritated and cross with group living, who wouldn't be? Not everybody wants to live with twenty-four other people, it's not an experience that you're ever faced with in normal life.'

'People say "my mother never used to swear", but you know they haven't learned that in dementia,' says Janet. 'Those are things they've picked up all their life and they're a little bit disinhibited now. And they've got a damned good reason to swear, you know?'

I can see the point, but still, it seems to me that a consistent set of personality traits is not a person. Janet's metaphors seem to get it exactly wrong. I am my baggage. I am the layers that have grown on the onion, not the tiny core at the middle. We are precisely all the things we've accrued, the memories, the experience, the learning. If you strip away what you call the baggage you're stripping away precisely the things that make us, that fill us out.

But if this is true, is it not perhaps a dangerous truth? Janet and Jackie are carers, and I have no doubt that if I had to entrust the care of a relative with dementia, or myself, to someone else, I'd like it to be to people who agree more with them than with me. As Jackie put it, 'The problem with seeing people as having no potential, or no insight, or as just a shell, is what's the point of bothering with somebody like that? What's the point of giving good care to somebody if they're just a shell? Unless you look at it in a positive light, somebody with dementia is never going to get the best care you could give them.'

And there is no doubt that the care Janet and Jackie give is excellent. They pioneered treatment without psychotropic medication, which in practice usually means sedation. Such care does not fit easily with phrases like 'the lights are off'. 'We would never say that,' says Janet. 'I don't think a good carer would say that.'

Whether or not Janet and Jackie hold the correct view of dementia and the self, their experience does perhaps provide some comfort for the many of us who fear dementia more than any other illness. 'There's this idea that you hear bandied around that people make living wills and if they get dementia then they want to be quietly put to sleep,' says Janet. 'All of our residents may have said that at one time, any one of them could have said that. But if you asked any one of them if they would like to die, they would say no.'

The reason is that dementia encroaches gradually, and it is remarkable what we can get used to if it happens by small enough increments. 'If you were to end up being eighty tomorrow you'd be mortified, but that doesn't happen, fortunately. You gradually age, you get a little more wrinkles here a little more wrinkles there, you look in the mirror and think, oh my god that's not me. With dementia, this is also a long process. It's something Robert will have compensated for in Linda for some long time before he even thought she had dementia. So that process has already started long before anybody knows about it. And it gradually becomes you.'

This is perhaps the most surprising truth about dementia. When I saw Robert with Linda, I found it hard to understand how the reality did not crush him. Try to imagine the person you love most in the world, someone bright, intelligent and vivacious, now unable to recognise you, muttering gibberish. I can't: it's too painful. But of course dementia progresses gradually and it is remarkable how much people adapt to it. As Janet said so eloquently, 'it gradually becomes you'. John Bayley captured something of this in his memoir of his wife, Iris Murdoch. Describing life in the late stages of her dementia, he writes, 'I cannot now imagine Iris any different. Her loss of memory becomes, in a sense, my own.'[12]

Therein lies a paradox of any view of the self which puts psychological continuity at its core. On such views, radical discontinuity destroys it. But if there is no hard core of self, and it is always in flux, then as long as the change is gradual, two very different stages in a person's life can legitimately be seen as stages in the life of one self. This explains the paradoxical position of the dementia sufferer, who is in some senses both still there and long gone.

Robert lives these paradoxes daily. In some ways, it is as though Linda has already died. 'I call it being half a widower,' he says. 'You're in an ambivalent condition, which is just one of the things you adapt to.

'It took me over eighteen months till the day came when I put all her clothes in plastic bags and took them up to the charity shop. Two months after she went into the home I *could* have made myself do it, but I wouldn't have *wanted* to do it, and that is a process of mourning. It was partly in anticipation of the fact that I was going to move, but moving house was part of the process of mourning ending. So yes, there's a process of mourning, and yes, I knew I was going through it, and yes, as far as it ever finishes, it's now finished.'

Talk of mourning is more than a figure of speech. It affects, for instance, the question of what someone in Robert's position would do if he met someone he might have a relationship with. 'I've been round this quite a lot,' he tells me. 'My so far abstract view of the matter – because it's not really become an issue with anybody – is I wouldn't see any external barriers to this. I've run this in front of my kids who are both in their thirties, and the message I get is, if you made a decision we wouldn't have any difficulty with it.'

I don't think many people would disagree. Another 'half widower', Bruce Bovill, spoke of his experience in starting a new relationship while his wife was in the advanced stages of Alzheimer's. He has moved in with his new partner and says he never once felt guilty and that the relationship helps him to care for his wife better. 'Jan is still my wife and I love her but it isn't the same love as we had. It can't be, because she has changed utterly.'[13]

So there is mourning, and the ending of the old form of relationship, perhaps even replaced by another. But that does not mean the old relationship is over. 'It's funny,' said Robert, 'there's a slightly sparky girl who worked at the place, who said to me one day, "Do you still love your wife?" I looked at her and said, "Of course."' Likewise, a reader wrote to the newsletter of the Alzheimer's Society to express outrage that 'a GP had told a man he was no longer married because his wife, who had dementia, did not know him and was as good as dead'.[14] What the GP said was in some sense true, but that truth was only one half of the paradox. As a friend once spoke of Linda to Robert, 'She may no longer know you, but you still know her.' But of what he stills knows, much has gone, much has changed, and little remains the same.

'Knowledge of what has happened to a person's body and its parts will not necessarily give you knowledge of what has happened to the person, so persons are not the same as their bodies.'

Richard Swinburne, theologian

4

Soul searching

The search for the pearl of self has so far been unsuccessful, but not fruitless. Some other picture of the self is emerging, one in which there may be no hard, stable core, but there is some real, albeit fragile, unity, based on memories and minds, embedded in an embodied brain. However, there is one possible candidate for the pearl of self that we have so far ignored: the soul. Many people believe that a human being, in addition to having a physical body, also has a non-physical part which does not depend on oxygen and food and which can persist long after our bodies have rotted into the earth. This soul is the true seat of the self: the body is merely a temporary vessel.

Some version of this idea probably is and has been the most common belief around the world through human history. One of the most popular and persuasive arguments for it was first formulated by the Persian philosopher Avicenna (*c.*980–1037). Avicenna's 'floating man' thought experiment asks the reader to 'imagine himself as though he is created all at once and created perfect, but that his sight has been veiled from observing external things, and that he is created falling in the air or the void in a manner where he would not encounter air resistance, requiring him to feel, and that his limbs are separated from each other so that they neither meet nor touch. He must then reflect as to whether he will affirm the existence of his self.'

The intuition almost everyone has is that we would indeed think that we existed in such a state of sensationless suspension. 'He will not doubt his affirming his self existing, but with this he will not affirm any limb from among his organs, no internal organ, whether heart or brain and no external thing. Rather, he would be affirming his self without affirming it for length, breadth, and depth.'

So far, so good. But what does this intuition tell us? Avicenna draws a startling conclusion. 'Hence the one who affirms has a means to be alerted to the existence of his soul as something other than the body – indeed, other than body – and to his being directly acquainted with [this existence] and aware of it.'[1]

The argument can be reconstructed in the following way. The floating man would be conscious of himself but not of his body. In order for this to be possible, there must be something other than his body for him to be conscious of. That means he must have a non-material part, a soul. Furthermore, this soul, not his body, must be who he really is, since it is the soul, not the body, which must always be present if he is to continue to exist.

This is a spectacular example of both how easily our intuitions can lead us astray, and how easy it is to draw false conclusions from them. First of all, what exactly is it that we are able to imagine in this case? To be precise, I would say it is a person with no awareness of her body or the physical space around her. Is this the same as imagining a self which is separate from the body? Or is it more like imagining one's body to be invisible and able to pass through material objects? Imagination seems to be somewhat unclear here.

Can you imagine having no body? It's important when considering this that you don't simply imagine being invisible and intangible. If you imagine yourself seeing and hearing things, from a particular point of view, for instance floating above the clouds, then you are imagining yourself located in space and time and so it is arguable that you are assuming some kind of physical presence. The challenge is a tougher one than this. Can you imagine yourself with no sensations or perceptions, in no particular time or space?

Some people when asked this, reply that of course they can. They can even get close to imagining it by closing their eyes in a quiet room and just focusing on their thoughts. Having no body would be like this: only being aware of thought and not of any sensory or other external stimuli. However, it seems unclear to me whether such people have successfully imagined *not having* a body or simply imagined *not being aware* of it.[2]

There is another way in which a sense of not being a body, even if we genuinely had it, could be wildly misleading. Something may experience itself to be one thing, while in fact being something quite different. Imagine someone in the grip of a psychedelic-drug-induced hallucination, convinced that he is a cockroach. Even if we allow that the experience is reported accurately – that the person really does feel and see his body to be that of a cockroach – it should be clear that he is in fact no such thing, but a freaked-out hippy. In just the same way, the mere fact that someone reports – even accurately – that he can experience himself as bodyless does not in any way prove that he is essentially a soul rather than a material substance.

There was a wonderful cartoon that circulated around university departments when I was an undergraduate that dramatised this fallacy beautifully. A thought bubble emerges from a computer. 'I think,' it says. In the next frame, 'I think, therefore I am.' *Cogito ergo sum*, in Descartes' memorable Latin phrase. The computer then goes on to continue a chain of thought that essentially follows that of Descartes, whose famous *cogito* argument shares the same basic logic as Avicenna's falling man. As a thinking thing, the computer concludes, as does Descartes, that it is this capacity for thought which defines what it is, and that other features, such as its metal case and silicon chips, do not comprise its essential nature. It is *res cogitans* – a thinking thing – not *res extensa* – an extended, material thing. Overjoyed by this discovery the computer starts dancing around, only to accidentally pull its plug out of the socket. The dancing and the thought bubbles abruptly cease.

Avicenna and Descartes made the same elementary mistake as the computer, as have most proponents of 'substance dualism' – the view that the world is made up of both physical matter and also some nonmaterial substance, mental or spiritual. But why is this apparently simple error so common? A convincing explanation was offered by Gilbert Ryle in his 1949 classic *The Concept of Mind*. Ryle accused dualists of making what he called a 'category mistake'. They started from the correct idea that thoughts, feelings and sensations were not physical things. The category mistake was to conclude that they must therefore be a different *kind of thing*, a non-physical thing. But there is another, more plausible alternative: they are not *things* at all. Rather, thinking and feeling are what brains and bodies *do*. Mind should not be thought of a substance, but as a kind of activity.

Category mistakes are encouraged by conventions of language. When a word used to describe something is a noun, it is tempting to think that the word it describes is an object of some kind. So, if 'mind' is a noun, then minds must be things. But all sorts of nouns are not physical things, yet we do not think that they are some kind of other, ghostly thing. You can't measure love in physical terms, despite the chuckles from a group of teenagers when I illustrated this point by saying it would not make sense to say 'my love for you is six inches long'. But no one would conclude that therefore love is a nonphysical object. Nor would denying it was such an object suggest you did not think it was real. Another example would be a song, which is not identical either with any written score nor any particular performance. A song is real, but it is not a physical or non-physical object.

Dualism's mistake is to argue that since minds, thoughts and feelings are not identical with any particular physical things, they must be non-physical things. Ryle compares this to thinking that since Oxford University is not the same as any particular college or building of the university, it must be another kind of building, whereas in fact it is not a single building at all. My favourite of Ryle's many examples is the person who understands that playing cricket requires team-spirit, but thinks that contributing team-spirit is an activity additional to batting, bowling and fielding, rather than being tied up with the manner of doing all of them.[3]

The weaknesses in the arguments for immaterial souls are so evident that most serious philosophers now agree with Ryle, who famously dismissed Descartes' notion as the myth of 'the ghost in the machine'. Indeed, as we'll see later, it is arguably not even the mainstream Christian view. But the traditional soul does still have some heavyweight defenders, most notably Richard Swinburne, who until his recent retirement was Nolloth Professor of the Philosophy of the Christian Religion at the University of Oxford, one of the most prestigious chairs in theology in the country. Swinburne is a Christian, but he claims that his arguments for the existence of the soul are purely rational and do not rest on his faith. More than that, he thinks rational arguments are the linchpins of his religious belief. 'The answer as to why I came to believe is that I haven't got a clue. But the answer as to why I now believe is on the basis of arguments, certainly.' He honestly believes that anyone who truly followed his chain of reasoning would have to accept its conclusion, be they religious or not. The fact that the vast majority of contemporary philosophers seem to be eminently qualified to follow his arguments yet reject them outright does not in any way seem to undermine his confidence in their robustness. 'The only reason people deny what stares them in the face is because they're captured by the physicalist dogma current in our time,' he told me when we met in his Oxford home.

Swinburne believes that souls are necessary to explain both the existence of consciousness and the identities of persons. One argument he uses starts from a thought experiment that has been used by many philosophers of mind over the last half decade. The scenario was inspired by Sperry and Gazzaniga's split-brain experiments which we looked at in Chapter Two. These seemed to show that each hemisphere of the brain could function as a distinct centre of consciousness without the other.[4] The thought experiment asks us to imagine what could happen *if* this – and some other rather fanciful technological advances – were possible, and if a brain could be divided in such a way that both halves could completely preserve the personality and memories of the unfortunate patient. You don't need to believe this is actually possible: whatever moral of the story you draw does not depend on it being any more than hypothetical.

So let us imagine that I am put under the knife of the kind of unethical neurosurgeon who could only make a living conducting the kind of bizarre operation favoured in philosophers' imaginations. He divides the two hemispheres of my brain and places each one in the bodies of two unfortunates whose own brains have been destroyed, but whose bodies have been kept alive. Call the one with my right hemisphere Rightian and the other Leftian. Both awake and both claim to be me. They both remember as much about my past as each other, and both have identical personalities. The question then is, which, if any, is me?

There are four possible answers: both, neither, Leftian or Rightian. Different philosophers have given different answers, but most agree on certain key points. The first is that it can't be the case that both are me. The reason for this is a simple logical one. If both are me then both must be the same person. But clearly they are not the same person: if you kill one, the other stays alive; if one watches *A Fistful of Dollars* in one room and the other watches *Blazing Saddles* in another, they have different experiences and acquire different memories. However you look at it, it cannot be literally true that both are me.

There is one interesting dissenting view. David Lewis and others argue that the best way to look at such cases is to say that we have one person whose life branches.[5] The rather prosaic analogy here is with a road that, at certain stages, divides into two, which may or may not rejoin several miles later. Although normally a road follows a single route, there is no conceptual difficulty in imagining one that does not. It is purely a matter of convention whether we give one branch a new name or simply talk of, say, the High Street (north) and High Street (south). Likewise, we could talk about Rightian and Leftian, but why not Julian (Right) and Julian (Left)?

This seems weirder than the road case, to be sure. But then the whole thought experiment is weird. It seems an odd objection to say that you're not allowed to describe an extraordinary occurrence in extraordinary terms. Although we normally assume that each person has only one stream of consciousness, this could be simply because, as a matter of fact, this just happens always to be the case.

Whether you accept Lewis's argument or not, there is an important point of agreement between him and most who take the alternative view. That is, the two people who come into existence by means of the hemisphere transplants have different and independent streams of consciousness, and therefore in an important respect they are two separate lives.

The second point most philosophers agree on is that it can't be that only one of either Rightian or Leftian is me. The reason for this is that both have an equal claim to be me, but neither has a better claim. To say that one is me and the other isn't would therefore be arbitrary. That leaves a general agreement that, in such a case, neither person is me.

What follows from this, however, is the subject of much dispute. The pivotal question here is, what would matter in such a case? Derek

Parfit argued that although in such cases there is no relation of identity between me and the future persons, both Rightian and Leftian give me 'what matters in survival'.[6] We will consider this radical claim in Part Two. For the moment, it's simply worth noting that the conclusion that neither Rightian nor Leftian would be me does necessarily not end my interest in their future lives.

Swinburne, however, does not accept that neither Rightian nor Leftian would be me. He argues that one must be. His argument is essentially this. In the split-brain case, we know all the physical facts about what has happened to me. However, we do not know, on the basis of these facts, which one, if either, is me. Nor would Rightian or Leftian be able to shed light on this, since both would claim to be me, and both could not be right. But Swinburne assumes one of them must be me, it's just that we don't know which it is. And since that answer is not determined by the physical facts, it must be determined by some non-physical facts. And for there to be such non-physical facts, we must have non-physical parts, ones which fix our identities. In short, we must have souls. As he summarises it, 'My argument has been that knowledge of what has happened to a person's body and its parts will not necessarily give you knowledge of what has happened to the person, and so, that persons are not the same as their bodies.'[7]

There are several questionable assumptions behind this line of argument. The first concerns the alleged inadequacy of a physical account of a person's life to explain everything about them. 'The trouble with physicalism,' Swinburne told me, 'is that it doesn't face the data, and the data first of all is the mental life. We have thoughts and feelings and so on and the occurrence of these does not entail the occurrence of goings on in the brain or conversely.' The conclusion is that a physical account of the world is not a complete account of the world. Therefore, there must be more to the world than the physical.

It should be clear that this argument simply repeats the kind of category mistake identified by Ryle. So it is true, as Swinburne says, that a physical account of the world is not a complete account of the world. But it does not follow that the world is comprised of more stuff than physical stuff. Rather, it simply follows that a complete account of the world is more than just an account of physical descriptions of the movements of stuff. This should not be a difficult thought. In the same way, a proper account of a game of football is not an account of the changing co-ordinates of the twenty-two players and the ball. If you knew enough about the game, such a description might enable you to infer what was going on, but nothing in it would entail that this was a sport with certain rules and a certain result.

Swinburne's first questionable move is to leap from the observation that a purely physical account of persons is not a complete account of persons to the conclusion that persons must therefore have non-physical parts. The second is that, in the split-brain case, there is a truth about what has happened to the person which we cannot know on the basis of the physical facts, namely, which of them is me. This is an example of what Derek Parfit calls a 'further fact' view of the self.[8] According to such theories, knowing all the facts about a person's brain, body, thoughts, feelings, relations and so on is never enough to tell you all there is to know about who the person is. There must be some further fact, perhaps a fact about which soul they possess, which is needed to settle such matters.

But why should we think such further facts exist? Nations provide an apt analogy here. A complete account of the lands, peoples and relations of a nation tell you everything about that nation. There are no further facts which make nations nations. It is true that wholes are greater than the sums of their parts, but that is not because wholes are additional, different kinds of parts. Persons are no exceptions. We are greater than the sums of our parts, but not because there is some further part left out of the sum. We are *nothing but* our parts, but we are *more than just* our parts.

All that is most importantly wrong in Swinburne's argument is therefore captured in his summary of it: 'knowledge of what has happened to a person's body and its parts will not necessarily give you knowledge of what has happened to the person, and so, persons are not the same as their bodies'. The first part is a questionable assumption. Knowledge of what has happened to a person's body and its parts may well give you all the knowledge you could have of what has happened to the person. Fatal to his argument, however, is the second part. 'Persons are not the same as their bodies' is true if it means that we are more than just our bodies, but that doesn't establish the existence of immaterial souls. It is just false, however, if it means we need more than the existence of our functioning bodies to be who we are.

Swinburne's commitment to the truth seems to be genuine, whatever his ability to arrive at it. So it is that, having argued that souls must exist, he thinks through the implications for this in rigorous detail, accepting them, no matter how bizarre they might seem. For instance, Swinburne insists that it is essential to start from the facts, and it has not escaped his notice that one cast-iron fact is that functioning brains and bodies are necessary for consciousness, at least in this life. It may be a logical possibility that there could be forms of consciousness in other worlds that do not depend on organic matter, but that doesn't seem to be the case in this one.

To this we need to add another compelling fact: if you have a sufficiently complex brain and body, you will be conscious. Combined with the first fact, most people would conclude that brains and bodies are both necessary and sufficient for human consciousness: you can't think or feel without them; and with them, as long as they're working properly, you can't but think and feel. Having committed himself to belief in souls, however, Swinburne can't accept this position. On his view, the non-material part of us is as essential as the material. No matter how complete our nervous systems are, without souls they couldn't think. But he also accepts that such bodies and brains are necessary for thought, so souls could not think without bodies either – at least not in this life. What God in his goodness might decide to make possible in the next life is anyone's guess. 'What I have argued,' he writes, '. . . is that without a functioning brain, the soul will not function (i.e. have conscious episodes) – not that it will not exist.'[9]

Swinburne uses the analogy of a light bulb to explain this. 'The soul is like a light bulb and the brain is like an electric light socket. If you plug the bulb into the socket and turn the current on, the light will shine. If the socket is damaged or the current turned off, the light will not shine. So, too, the soul will function (have a mental life) if it is plugged into a functioning brain.'[10] But, like a magician, it is always possible that God could cause an unplugged bulb to light up if he so wanted: 'maybe there are other ways of getting souls to function other than plugging them into brains'.

This analogy ironically shows how far materialist conceptions have come, since it is the mirror image of a much older view: that it is the body which requires animating by an immaterial soul. The philosopher Avicenna, for instance, thought that the soul animated and controlled the body, even though it did not come into existence before it.[11] That even a dualist today accepts that bodies power souls and not vice versa is indicative of widespread belief in the materialist basis of the world.

So what follows from Swinburne's view? First, that 'I don't think that persons necessarily come into existence only by means of sexual activity'. Souls have to be put there too. Nevertheless, if a person had the right kind of brain and body, she would also have a soul. By some divine fiat, every functioning electrical light socket is granted a light bulb. So, if we produced a synthetic human, or even a computer that had enough sophistication to sustain consciousness, somehow, every such thing would indeed have a soul.

How does that happen? Swinburne doesn't know. 'I can't explain what causes my foetus to produce a subject of experience but it's a datum that it does. I can't provide an explanation for how when you make your highly sophisticated computer, what would cause it to produce as I would say a soul, but still it would do so.' This explanatory gap doesn't bother him. 'The world is full of things that scientists have observed and they haven't got the slightest idea how to explain them, but that doesn't cast doubt on the data.' Nevertheless, Swinburne does have some idea as to why it is that all bodies, or even computers, capable of having souls plugged into them do in fact have souls plugged into them. 'If there's a God, he has an interest in producing conscious beings.' God wants as many souls to flicker into life as possible, and so is quite happy to go around plugging them into whatever soul-sockets pop into existence.

Swinburne's view is a prime example of the limits of the virtue of consistency. He does work very hard to make sure that all its bits fit together. But so many of those bits are just wildly implausible. There is no good reason to think that functioning brains and bodies need souls plugged into them if they are to give rise to thoughts. There is no good reason to believe that our inability to provide a simple answer to the question of who the results of a split-brain operation are means that there must be some non-physical fact that would answer it. And there is no good reason to suppose that the existence of facts about the world that cannot be fully described in the language of physics means that there are substances in the world that are not physical.

Swinburne is not the only serious thinker to advocate the existence of non-material souls, of course. But he is one of the most eminent, and his account is one of the most systematic and thorough. His writings lay bare the logic of dualistic souls, and once exposed, its failings should be obvious. Swinburne shows how it is possible to maintain a rigorously consistent view of non-material souls, even while accepting much of the scientific knowledge that tells us that having a mental life depends on functioning brains and bodies. But it is not enough for a view to be consistent: it must rest on good arguments and evidence that the view is the best explanation for what it is trying to explain. Swinburne believes his view is such a best explanation, but I cannot agree that the only reason he is in a small minority is because the majority are in the grip of atheist and materialist dogmas. Put simply, they recognise bad arguments when they see them, and Swinburne's are often very bad indeed, resting on a basic category mistake and the drawing of a bizarre conclusion from split-brain thought experiments.

There are other arguments for the existence of souls, of course. But if you're looking for gold, there has to come a point where you stop digging fruitlessly in one spot and move on to another. To switch metaphors, if the soil is not proving to be fertile, it is better to plant elsewhere than to continue in the hope that persistence will bear fruit. In all my years of reading and thinking about soul and self, I've yet to come across a single argument that is left standing after even a little serious scrutiny. As an idea, the immaterial soul is dead, and it's time we buried it, along with any other dreams we might have had about finding the pearl at the heart of our identity.

PART TWO

Constructions

It may seem premature to give up the search for the pearl of self so soon. But the truth is that even my swift overview of the main candidates gives more credence to the pearl view than most serious investigators of the self would nowadays think fair. As we have seen, virtually no psychologists and very few contemporary philosophers believe that there is such a core to be found within us. As has been suggested, but not yet fully explained, our unity is a product of various parts and processes working together. Unity is the product of the self system, it is not the basis of it.

What this means, in broad terms, is that you, me and everyone else are in some sense constructions, of mind and of matter. Many will find this troubling. If we are constructions, then could we not have been constructed differently? Might we not reconstruct or even deconstruct ourselves? Could it be that we are who we are simply because society has formed us in a certain, arbitrary way? Without a pearl, does the self simply dissolve into a million parts, with nothing to hold it together? Does embracing the notion that persons are constructions actually lead to the destruction of all we hold dear about ourselves?

'I'd say if you have too healthy an appreciation for who you are, that leaves you open to fossilising yourself. Everything's open to revision.'

Brooke Magnanti, a.k.a. Belle de Jour

5

Multiplication

Once upon a time, in a castle on a large hill, there lived eleven strange, fractious individuals. There was Bobby, a 'naughty imp' who liked playing jokes and roller-blading but who was often kept locked in the dungeon by Tommy, an angry young man prone to fits of anger and violence. Wanda was a kind, insightful woman, who nevertheless had previously been the malicious Witch. Robbey was the young high-achiever who nonetheless could not meet the expectations of his parents. It was he who did all the hard work that enabled Bob, the sensible one, to become a successful expert on the East, and a former president of the Asia Society. Young Bob just sat on the castle walls, playing his flute. Up in the tower was Eyes, who saw everything but said nothing. The Librarian kept the secrets of the castle locked up, including the darkest one of all: that Baby was the victim of persistent sexual abuse. And trying to make sense of all this was Robert.

The castle and all its inhabitants were contained within the head of one man: Robert B. Oxnam. Oxnam was diagnosed with Dissociative Identity Disorder (DID), more commonly, but anachronistically, known as Multiple Personality Disorder. In his account of his life with DID, *A Fractured Mind*, Oxnam tells an incredible tale of how, through therapy, all these different 'alters' – as the different personalities are known – first came to light and how they then became at least partially integrated, so that only Bobby, Robert and Wanda remained, functioning in unison.

In 1990, Bob was in a bad way. Although he was a very successful, respected academic, he was trying to deal with alcoholism, bulimia and depression. Perhaps most worryingly, over the last decade, he had increasingly experienced memory blanks. 'Sometimes, when a luncheon appointment was cancelled, I would go out at noon and come back at 3 p.m. with no knowledge of where I had been or what I had done.'[1] On one business trip to Taiwan when a whole series of meetings was cancelled, he had no idea what he had done for three days, although he did emerge from the blank with a terrible headache and cigarette burns on his arms.

Then one day an hour-long psychotherapy session came to an end when Bob thought it had only just started. His therapist, Dr Jeffrey Smith, revealed that for the last fifty minutes, an angry young man who called himself Tommy had been talking to him. Bob had not physically left the room, but it seems he had left his body, and Tommy had taken over. Over the coming years, in sessions with Smith, nine more alters emerged, and along with them a whole mythology surrounding the castle. None of these alters was aware of the thoughts or actions of any of the others. Each was like a self-contained individual. It was as if each took a turn to hold the baton of consciousness, which could only be held by one hand at a time. After passing it on, they would skulk back into the recesses of the unconscious, affecting the life of Robert B. Oxnam in more mysterious ways.

That, at least, is how Oxnam and Smith understand it. But DID is a controversial disorder. It has been listed in the *Diagnostic and Statistical Manual* (*DSM*) of the American Psychiatric Association since its third edition in 1980, but that in itself proves little, since it also included homosexuality until 1973 and currently considers 'parent–child relational problem' to be a diagnosable condition. In the decade following its inclusion in *DSM*-III, the number of reported cases of DID shot up from 200 to around 4,000.[2]

According to Smith, and many other DID experts, the vast majority of cases begin with severe childhood abuse. Dissociation is essentially a coping mechanism for tolerating the intolerable. In a strange way it is entirely rational. If you have the thought 'this can't be happening to me', the logical corollary of this is 'this is happening to someone else'. If you think 'I can't bear this', then conjure up somebody else to cope with it for you. Most of us are familiar with less extreme versions of strategies like this. The introvert who hates social functions may create an outgoing persona, a pretence that can just be kept up long enough to get through the horrors of a hosting a dinner party. Someone who has to do an unpleasant job can see putting on their work clothes – or taking them off – as representing a line between the real self and a role that has to be taken on.

In most such cases, the roles we take on are clearly understood as roles. There is no radical dissociation between the 'real self' and the temporary facade. What makes DID qualitatively different is that the separation goes right to the bottom of the conscious self. A 'memory barrier' is erected between the alters, so that the memories, thoughts and actions of the alters become entirely separated from each other. So in the paradigmatic case, the victim of the abuse becomes an alter whose experiences and painful memories are not shared with the other alter or alters.

The strategy only works up to a point, however. It is hard work for the mind to keep each alter separate. What's more, the only way to do so is to divide up the self's resources. So one alter may get the creativity, another the discipline, which means that each one is deprived of a whole series of strengths. This means that the dominant alter, the one that is conscious for most of the time and which presents the public face of the individual, is often seriously dysfunctional.

That is a sketch of the believers' tale. There are, however, many who doubt DID really exists. The most serious worry concerns the way in which therapists bring alters to the surface. The deep philosophical question here is most evident when you consider the memories of childhood trauma that therapists elicit: how could anyone possibly know if what the client says about childhood abuse is a real memory or a confabulation? It is important here to remember that confabulation in this sense has nothing to do with deliberately lying or making things up. The mind confabulates any time that it comes up with a story of an event which didn't actually happen. As we saw in Chapter Three when we looked at memory, the human mind is a prolific confabulator. What's more, it is remarkably easy to elicit specific confabulations, as we saw from Elizabeth Loftus's Bugs Bunny experiments. That was Loftus's most famous study but in fact her work on false memory has spanned almost her entire career, and her case rests on an impressive body of data.

The idea that the unreliability of memory means that we cannot automatically trust recovered accounts of childhood abuse is one which generates a lot of hostility, especially from people who are or believe themselves to be victims of abuse. But work by Loftus and those like her is not part of some abuse-denying conspiracy. Doubts about the reliability of memory should not be confused with doubts about the reality of childhood sexual abuse. Nor should a belief that some, if not many, recovered memories of abuse are false entail that all or most memories of abuse are. Unfortunately, however, the debate over how best to understand cases of apparent DID is too often fought along crude abuse-deniers-versus-victims lines. Oxnam's therapist makes just this mistake, claiming that 'the controversies surrounding multiple personality have the same source as the disorder itself: the very human wish to avoid acknowledging overwhelming helplessness and pain'.[3]

This argument actually shows just what is suspect in the clinical methodology that leads to diagnosis of DID. The psychoanalytic method is premised on the idea that the client is not only unconscious of certain key facts about herself, but that she will often also positively deny these truths. Within this dynamic, the client is in the same paradoxical situation as the mistaken messiah in Monty Python's *Life of Brian*. Denial of divinity is taken to confirm it, but assertion of divinity is taken to be confirmation, not denial. Whatever he says confirms the thesis. In the same way, if a therapist believes the client has suffered abuse, then denial will be taken to indicate repression, while assertion will be a sign that this repression has been overcome. Given that childhood abuse is taken by DID believers to be the usual cause of the disorder, this dynamic is very often likely to occur. And given that there is increasing evidence that people can be made to 'remember' things that never happened, there is good reason to at least refuse to take at face value the evidence that DID sufferers were mostly abused.

Confabulation is not only a potential problem when it comes to causes, however. Could it also be that the alters are themselves *brought into being* by the therapeutic process, rather than simply *brought to light* by them? Reading Oxnam's account, the possibility certainly seems plausible. The problem is again one of knowing how even to distinguish between pre-existing alters and ones that have been made up. Because confabulation is not wilful lying, not even the client herself could know whether or not the alter she becomes aware of for the first time has been inhabiting her brain for years or has just popped into existence.

It is certainly beyond my competence and the scope of this book to pronounce on this issue. The only thing I am confident about is that it is far too simplistic to see the choice being between accepting DID as real, exactly as described by *DSM*, or dismissing it as a lot of nonsense. It is possible, for instance, that dissociation is very real, that people can create 'memory barriers' between different phases of their lives and that they may behave differently when within one set of walls than another. All that could be true while at the same time also being true that the rich, rounded personalities attributed to alters, along with many specific memories, are all or mostly confabulations. In other words, alters may be confabulations created to make sense of the reality of dissociation.

My main interest, however, is not in settling the controversy over DID, but in what its very possibility tells us about ordinary personal identity. If the pearl view of the self were true, it would be hard even to make sense of multiple personalities. Whether Robert B. Oxnam was telling it as it is or confabulating, his book would not be coherent. But, for the most part at least, it is. Even if we find it implausible or incredible, his account is possible.

The model by which it makes sense can be explained by analogy to a normal desktop computer. Many computers are shared, so when you switch one on, you have to log on as a particular user. When you do that, you enter a virtual space which has a 'memory barrier' between you and other users. You cannot access their files and they can't access yours. On some systems, different users also have access to different functions. So, for instance, you could only allow internet access to yourself and older children, or you could for some reason deny others use of your image-manipulation software.

It should be clear how this analogy applies to the self. Our hardware is the brain and body, with the brain functioning as the processor (CPU). The 'software' is how the system has come to be 'wired up'. Each person's neural networks are connected differently, which is why you and I may have essentially the same brains, but I have my memories, knowledge and so on and you have yours. But there is nothing which says that all the billions of different neural connections need to be equally accessible at the same time. Indeed, we know that they are not. What we can remember or do can vary considerably depending on our situation, something we'll return to shortly.

On the computer model, the alters of someone with DID are like different users. Robert Oxnam would sometimes 'log on' as Bob, sometimes as Tommy, sometimes as Wanda, and so on. Each of these alters had a different 'user profile', granting them access to different memories and functions. Of course, this is only an analogy and it's not perfect. Most obviously, no one consciously ever logs on or off: the switching is more automatic that that. Nevertheless, the basic principle of multiple users of the same system is the same in both the computer case and that of supposed DID.

This could just about make sense on a pearl view of the self. It could be that the material or spiritual core of the self could be erased and reloaded with the settings of each alter at each switching. But this sounds implausible and cumbersome. It all makes much more sense if we reject the pearl view. If there is no single place in the brain where it all comes together, then the set of memories, dispositions and so on that the individual had conscious access to at any one time could change quite easily. It's a bit like a picture made up of hundreds of black and white dots. It could be that 90 per cent of the dots are identical, but the 10 per cent that differ create a totally different image.

The only thing needed to radically change the way in which the self operates and sees itself is for some parts of the system to become dormant (or less active) while others become (more) active.

To put it in broader terms, the self is not a single thing, it is simply what the brain and body system does. If that's so, then there is absolutely no reason in principle why the brain couldn't do different things at different times. In that sense, as the philosopher Daniel Dennett and the psychologist Nicholas Humphry concluded in their investigation into DID, not only is multiplicity 'biologically and psychologically possible' but 'the possibility of developing multiple selves is inherent in every human being'.[4]

This inherent possibility should, I think, be accepted. However, it raises a broader question. The kind of extreme dissociation in DID may be rare, or even non-existent, but if the self lacks a fixed core and is flexible enough to in principle be multiple, then should we think of ourselves in ordinary life as having significant dimensions of multiplicity? Once the idea of the unitary self is fractured, should we not take this one stage further and accept that in the absence of a strongly singular 'I', there must be a weakly multiple 'we'?

Madonna and whore

Although most people find the idea of multiple-personality disorder strange and alien, many, perhaps the majority, buy into a weaker idea of multiplicity. For instance, there is a reason why these lines from Walt Whitman's 'Song of Myself' have become so widely quoted:

> Do I contradict myself?
> Very well then I contradict myself,
> (I am large, I contain multitudes.)

Many, if not most, people believe that they are multi-faceted, and that people who only know them in one specific context are not seeing the full picture. Although it is true that a great number take pride in saying that 'what you see is what you get', many others will tell you that there is more to them than meets the eye.

However, this weak idea that we are multi-faceted seems light years away from saying we are in some deep sense multiple. So what makes some take that extra step and say that it is not so much that we have different sides to our selves, but that we have different selves? One of the most fashionable drivers behind the idea that we should all think of ourselves as multiple rather than singular is postmodernism. The nature of 'postmodernism' is hard to pin down, not least because it is in part a denial of the apparently old-fashioned idea that any reality can be pinned down, or even that there is such a thing as reality to be pinned down. It is, however, possible to say some general things about postmodernism which explain why it makes such a good bedfellow for the view of self as multiple.

If postmodernism has a unifying theme it is one of fragmentation, which it picked up from modernism and ran with wildly. This is most evident in postmodern architecture. Until its emergence, there had been numerous styles of building, but each had a particular style, unity and identity. A church could be Norman, classical, neoclassical, gothic, rococo, modernist and so on. Postmodernism rejected these neat distinctions. Architectural styles do not come pre-packaged with particular essences that cannot be mixed. Rather, you can take the distinctive features of each style, throw in some new innovations for good measure, and shuffle them up like a pack of cards. Why not have Doric columns, gothic windows and modernist doors? In fact, why should one building only have one style of anything? Why not a Doric arch, a couple of Corinthians, a Romanesque and a few Ionics?

This is not fragmentation for fragmentation's sake, however. Underlying it is an intellectual rejection of various kinds of essentialism or realism. Before postmodernism, so we are told, most dominant modes of thought took reality to have a single, real essence. Science, for instance, attempted to investigate the cosmos as it is and to represent a unified, single form of understanding that penetrated the essence of the material world. Geography mapped the world, and the competition between cartographical conventions would be settled by which one mapped it most accurately. History was the story of what has happened, and was successful when it unearthed the truth about what really happened.

Postmodernism rejected all that. The world has no real essence that is just waiting for us to describe. Reality is constituted by our understanding of it. History is created by the stories we tell about the past, and there are innumerable different such stories we can tell about the same events. Likewise, the Earth can be mapped differently: you don't even need to privilege the land surface. Science is also a collection of stories we tell ourselves, ones we value for their instrumental or perhaps aesthetic value, but not because they reveal the essence of the real world.

These ideas can be captured in the idea of the rejection of grand or meta-narratives. Humans make sense of their world by telling stories. Meta-narratives are the big stories that tie everything together. The grand narrative of history provides a single, coherent story to explain the past; the grand narrative of science is the single story of the physical world; and so on. But these grand narratives are all false, because they impose a unified, singular structure on a world which has no fixed essence. In their place we need a multiplicity of narratives, ones which capture the different, contradictory perspectives that people in different times and places have of the world.

This analysis applies to the self as much as it does to anything else. The self has no immutable essence. Rather, it is constructed, like a fiction. But what is doing this constructing? It depends on which postmodernist you ask. The answer is often 'discourses': the ways in which language shapes thought and perpetuates power relations. A woman's identity, for instance, is 'constituted' by the discourses of her time which tell her how a woman should be. 'You and I are mere "sites" of such conflicting languages of power,' writes Seyla Benhabib, 'and "the self" is merely another position in language.'[5] A human being is 'not a unity, not autonomous, but a process,' says Catherine Belsey, 'perpetually in construction, perpetually contradictory, perpetually open to change'.[6] However, with this comes the promise of a liberation. If the self is constructed, then may we now take over the task of construction for ourselves? We can create ourselves, become the authors of our identities, writing as many of them as we want, not limiting ourselves to a singular identity.

Everyone really needs to calm down. Postmodernists seem to me like thinkers who have tasted potent conceptual liquor and, lacking all moderation, have become intellectual dipsomaniacs. Drunk on the rejection of totalising narratives, they fail to notice they have simply replaced them with a different one: the narrative that understands everything in terms of constitution by language and power. Taken to its logical conclusion, postmodernism itself would simply be one narrative among others, constituted by the discourses of its time, and no more worthy of respect than any other system of thought.

Many of the ideas at the root of their thinking are perfectly true, and we've come across many of them already: it is true that the self has no fixed essence, that it is in part a construction and that the autobiographical narratives we tell ourselves invent an order and cohesion that real lives lack. But it is not good enough to revel in this in a kind of Dionysian frenzy. You have to soberly think through what follows from it. And what does not follow is the opposite extreme. If you reject the singular grand narrative, it does not follow that we should embrace an infinity of contradictory narratives. The philosopher Bernard Williams nailed this fallacy beautifully when he wrote, 'As Clemenceau famously said at Versailles to a German who had wondered what future historians would say about all this, "They won't say that Belgium invaded Germany."[7]

So it is with the self. The problem with the postmodern conception of the self is that the fragmentation it sees is more of a theoretical necessity than an empirical reality. Look at real selves and you'll see that they are not 'merely' constructions of discourses or 'perpetually' contradictory. Indeed, I think being a fly on the wall at a postmodern theorist's breakfast would be enough to establish that. Each morning would not bring radical doubt about how that person would react to the news on the radio, what she would eat or drink, what she would be wearing and so on. The hyperbole of hyper-malleability is refuted by the simple observation that human beings, postmodernists included, display a remarkable amount of continuity and unity, even though they have no fixed essence.

The postmodern exaggeration of fragmentation leads to the overstatement of all kinds of ordinary ways in which we are multi-faceted. The prime example here is Madonna, the pop icon of postmodernism. To one writer, she is a 'polyvalent artist' who 'methodically discovered and constructed herself', 'tirelessly plays with signifiers' and wears 'different masks'. She 'celebrates the collapse of metanarratives' and 'favours the confusion of identities, propagates and multiplies ambiguities'.[8] There is some sense in which all of this is true. But it would be a mistake to think that all this meant that Madonna was, to use another modish phrase, 'radically decentred'. Overexcited academics seem to forget the essential point that Madonna is a *performer*. If you think the range of diverse personae she has adopted reveals deep truths about the nature of her self, then Sir Alec Guinness must be an even more important postmodern icon. After all, in one single 1949 film, *Kind Hearts and Coronets*, he played eight parts, one of them female.

A more recent example of a woman whose adoption of different identities might cause postmodernists to get overexcited is Dr Brooke Magnanti. Here we have a wonderful threefold division of identity. Magnanti is an academic researcher into developmental neurotoxicology and cancer epidemiology who once worked under another, unknown name, as a prostitute. For eighteen months between 2003 and 2004 she lived an archetypal 'double life', mostly studying for a PhD on informatics, epidemiology and forensic science, but sometimes getting paid £200 an hour as a 'high-class hooker'. In fact, it is more accurate to say she led a triple life, because under the nom de plume Belle de Jour, she blogged about her sex work and went on to publish two books based on this material. Three personae – Brooke, Belle and the happy hooker. Surely then, a paradigmatic example of a 'polyvalent self', freely constructing her own multiple identities?

Reading *Belle's Best Bits*, a kind of greatest hits collection from her two volumes of blogs, I quickly suspected not. It seemed Magnanti went into this line of work because it suited her. She sounded sexually experimental, easily able to divorce the erotic and the emotional, and pretty keen to do so. And when, in a Bristol pub not far from where Magnanti works, she told me about how she viewed her experiences, my suspicions became convictions.

Waiting for her to appear, as you are now, it was almost impossible not to construct some kind of image of what she would look like. Human beings think in terms of stereotypes, for good reasons. Without mental short cuts, we simply couldn't get by. There is just too much information to process, and we often have to be quite crude as to how we filter it. But these generalisations are bound to lead us astray. One illustrative psychology study, for instance, showed that if subjects were presented with lists of character traits for people labelled 'doctor', 'artist', 'skinhead' and 'estate agent', they later remembered those that fitted the stereotype more than they did those that confounded them.[9]

Stereotyping is also linked to false ideas of essence. Being a 'builder', for instance, is not just a description of your job, it's an indicator of your core identity. People often readily take on this essentialism for themselves. A label like 'mother' or 'manager' becomes not just one thing that you are, but your defining role. This ties identity too much to what is impermanent and fragile, as can be seen in the mother who hangs on too tightly to that role when her children have grown up, or the manager who loses self-respect when he is fired.

It is also problematic when others define us by such labels. For many, Brooke Magnanti is now for ever known as a prostitute, as though this captured her essence. 'It's an uphill struggle to get to talk to people about anything other than prostitution,' she says. 'Getting me to talk about prostitution is like asking someone who worked in McDonald's for a year and a half to talk about the global meat industry.'

Another example of the force of stereotypes is that I bet most readers are waiting for me to tell them what she looked like, more than they would have wanted descriptions of many of the other interviewees in this book. But why is that? I don't think it's just prurient curiosity at what a real-life high-class prostitute looks like. I suspect it has something to do with a feeling that how she looks will provide some clue as to how she could have lived this curious double life and what effect it had on her. But it doesn't. Like most people, she is neither stunningly beautiful nor completely plain. Her shoulder-length hair is wayward-straight with blonde highlights, parted unfussily on the right-hand side. Asked to guess her age, you'd probably come up with something around the true figure of thirty-four. 'Invariably, I can tell from people's reactions when they meet me for the first time that I'm never what anyone's actually expecting, even if they have a photo of me,' she says. 'I used to play this game of being on the Tube and thinking, "if someone walked in here, how long would they take to get to me, if they were looking for me? How many other people would they pick out first?" I came about sixth or seventh usually.'

Of course, one reason why photos, and with them purely physical descriptions, don't prepare us for the real person is that faces and bodies are animated, and how we carry ourselves contributes a lot to how we are perceived. Magnanti – when I met her at least – came over as ironic, a little wry, very straightforward and not one to worry too much about anything that can wait. You might well conclude she was playful, but you'd have no particular reason to think her sensual.

On reflection, none of this should be surprising. But it is remarkable how much of what we believe is impervious to reflection. In the case of Magnanti, it seems that people's rather crude expectations do indeed lead them to make the kind of unfounded assumptions that lead to false attributions of duality. The banal reality is that the maintenance of different identities does not go deep to the core of Magnanti's soul, but was simply a necessary means of keeping up some barriers for reasons of confidentiality and privacy. Most obviously, there is nothing philosophically profound about the fact she didn't use her real name for her sex work: 'Well, yeah, you just don't. That's not something anybody does.' It's just a name. 'At home nobody calls me Brooke. The name that I'm known by to my friends and family, that's not Brooke. I'm Brooke because that's the name that goes on the papers that get published in my work, but I don't think those are a disintegrated set of people.'

Nor did going to work require her to 'get into character', to become a different person. 'It wasn't really a character so much as just suppressing some things and bringing other things to the fore. It wasn't really playing a character because it was me. I mean, I remember having a conversation with a client once about chemoinformatics – that's definitely me. It's a bit like when you're giving a talk at a conference and you're wearing something you wouldn't normally wear: if you're a girl you put on a bit more make-up than you would usually wear, and then you only talk of x. It's like for that piece of time you're just a mouthpiece for your work and everything else about you is just too much, you leave the rest of that at the door. To what extent do people just pretty much do that in their lives? On the way home, I'm going to stop at the corner shop and get some milk, I'm not going to then sit there and tell my life story to the person behind the counter and I don't expect him to see me as anything other than a customer.'

Whatever you think about Magnanti's job choices, she seems to me to have a realistic grasp of how her identity is not rigidly fixed, but nor is she infinitely malleable, an open field of possibilities. 'There are constraints.' She nonetheless, wisely, only agrees that she has a healthy sense of who she is 'with caution'.

'I'd say if you have too healthy an appreciation for who you are, that leaves you open to fossilising yourself. Everything's open to revision. I'm an atheist, but let's face it, if there was a real God-created miracle out there right now, that would be open to revision. I'm not too attached to that as a definition of myself. I'm too much of a scientist to say that anything *is*.'

Magnanti was able to live her triple life, not because she was able to flip between different selves, but because she was at ease with the different features of her one self. So when people ask how she managed the difficulty of living with her different personae and roles, the question is misguided. 'I think anyone who asks that question is probably not aware of the extent to which they adjust what they're representing to the rest of the world. People have this fantasy of "I give 100 per cent of myself to the world, all the time." And online they also have this fantasy of "when I choose to hide things about myself that's completely undetectable to every other human". That's not the case.'

Others, however, have sometimes seen her differently. And as this story shows, how others see us can change the way we think of ourselves.

'My now obviously ex-boyfriend was very keen to represent me as though there was a good me and a bad me. Anything that I did that he liked – you know, I knit – that was good Brooke, and then if I behaved in a way he didn't like that was bad Brooke, as if there were two of me. It was like, "I know there is this good person. Why can't you be her all the time?" And I felt really uncomfortable with that, because when you're around someone a lot it's hard not to start to take on the way that they see you and what they've created as who you are, and you do kind of respond to certain things about that. At the beginning that wasn't the way I thought about it. It was more like going to work, putting on a suit; going to a party, putting on a dress; talking about x conversations, talking about y conversations. Then as time went on I did start to get the feeling, what if there's a good Brooke and a bad Brooke, and can I just uncover good Brooke? But then after I got out of that I thought back around it again and just thought if you took all these things that he had identified as this other person, this incredible me that I could be, there wasn't actually enough there to make a person: she does a lot of knitting and she really likes Radio Four, but there wasn't much else to her. And that was part of the whole decision with coming out: these bits need to be reintegrated now. It isn't working to try to be different people.'

Two things in particular strike me as revealing about how Magnanti tells this story. First, I think she identifies a general problem when she says that 'there wasn't actually enough there to make a person'. If we start to think about the different facets of ourselves as different people, we actually make each self or persona less than a full person. To be a whole person is precisely to have depth and more than one side. This is why DID is a disorder rather than a fascinating, postmodern way to live: each alter does not actually have enough to be a fully rounded individual.

Secondly, the way in which Magnanti adopted her ex-boyfriend's misguided way of thinking about her is a warning about how it really does matter how we conceptualise the contradictions and variations within us. In a sense, this shows how the postmodernists were right: there is nothing inevitable about the way we think about the world. We can carve it up in many different ways. What they fail to stress, though, is that some carvings-up are better and more truthful than others. We can indeed think of ourselves as pluralities, but in doing so we lose more than we gain.

It is significant, however, to realise just how much scope we do have to change the way we think about ourselves. As Wittgenstein said, 'Now were Dr Jekyll and Mr Hyde two persons or were they the same person who merely changed? We can say whichever we like. We are not forced to talk of a double personality.'[10] But although we can indeed 'say whichever we like', in some cases one way of speaking may be less misleading than another. When facts can be described in two different ways, one may be better, even if the other is not wrong. I have argued that it is unhelpful and misleading, for the majority at least, to think of ourselves as multiple rather than multifaceted. But that does not mean that it is incoherent to do so.

Mundane multiplicity

There is a minority which finds talk of multiplicity natural and preferable. You can find such people hanging out on websites like Astraeas Web and Collective Phenomenon.[11] These people claim to be multiple or 'co-conscious'. That simply means that they believe there is more than one person in their one body, and that this is not pathological. A lot of their efforts are directed at rejecting the idea that they are suffering from Dissociative Identity Disorder but are in denial. In particular, they reject the idea that being multiple is necessarily a result of childhood abuse or trauma. Nevertheless, this 'normal multiplicity' is very much like DID except in one very important respect. As one co-conscious multiple put it, 'The different alters are aware of the others, share and pass along information, and can even see what goes on if they choose, when they are not the person out in control of the body.'[12]

I'm a little sceptical. No doubt those who believe themselves to be co-conscious are sincere, but at the moment their claims remain untested. Nonetheless, the mere fact that there are people who claim to be co-conscious shows that the sense of being strongly unified is not universal. It's a reminder that one of the problems of talking about the subjective sense of self is that it is easily assumed that it is the same for everyone. Could it not rather be the case that the extent to which we perceive ourselves as one or many is in fact highly variable? That's what the science writer Rita Carter came to believe after researching her book *Multiplicity*.

'Multiplicity is a spectrum,' she told me when I caught up with one of her selves near their home in Oxfordshire. 'At the very extreme you have people with multiple-personality disorder who jump totally from one discrete personality to another. At the other end you have people who are almost entirely integrated, so that you can cut, slice them at any time, meet them in any context, and you will see the same recognisable things. I think both of those extremes are rare and most of us cluster in the middle.'

In support of this claim, Carter cites a very powerful weapon: empirical evidence. One of her biggest guns is state-dependent memory. 'In different mind-states one does not have access to the same bag of memories, and that has been demonstrated in a lot of quite clever studies. So when you are very angry you do not have access to the same memories that you have when you are feeling very benign and relaxed.' The research on this is extensive and well established. If you want to remember an event or fact, it is better to be in the same situation or state as you were when the event took place or when you learned the fact. There is even some evidence that something learned when drunk is better remembered when drunk than sober.[13] Not only memories, but skills and personality traits are often to some extent state-dependent. A familiar example, in the literal sense, is that no matter what their adult personality is, many people revert to childhood versions of themselves when they gather together as family.

So, argues Carter, you 'look at an individual person and talk about their personality, and what is it today and what is it tomorrow, and when you do that, you find that people do change dramatically, to the extent that in a normal way of speaking you would not refer to that person as the same entity in two different situations. Therefore, it seems to me that to talk about multiple personalities is more realistic, closer to what you're looking at, than to talk about a fuzzy, plastic, changeable, dynamic personality that nevertheless remains the same entity throughout.'

In other words, it is true that we could talk of multiple selves or multi-faceted selves, but the former is just more truthful than the latter. She illustrates this with the analogy of the self as a gemstone. 'If you accept the intuitive model, that of a many-faceted gem, a cut diamond rotating and catching different facets of light, the trouble with that is that it implies there is something underneath the faces, that there is a central core that is rotating the faces around. I'm saying something very different. I'm saying that if you take away the faces there is nothing in the centre.'

I am reminded of a recurrent analogy in Buddhist thought, in which the self is compared to a cart or chariot. A saying attributed to Sister Vagirâ, a contemporary of the Buddha, is: 'Just as it is by the condition precedent of the co-existence of its various parts that the word "chariot" is used, just so is it that when the *Skandhas* [aggregates] are there we talk of a "being".'[14] This is sometimes taken to mean that chariots do not exist, only their parts. But this is clearly nonsense. A cart is not an illusion just because it has no existence other than by the correct arrangement of its parts. The only thing that doesn't exist is an object which is somehow independent of its parts. In the same way, the self clearly exists, it is just not a thing independent of its constituent parts.

Likewise, on Carter's analogy, even if there is nothing left of a gem if you take away its facets, it is still a multi-faceted gem. The only problem is if you make the mistake of thinking of it as a single entity with a solid core that is separable from the facets. And this is where I think talk of multiplicity repeats the error it is trying to correct. The problem with our intuitive sense of self is that it excessively 'reifies': it makes a singular *thing* out of it. Multiplicity does exactly the same, only at a lower level: making singular, unified things out of the parts which make up the self. This seems even more misleading than the reification of the whole self: at least 'person' in the ordinary, intuitive sense is singular in several important ways, such as having a single body and a single autobiography. If it really is a mistake to think of the self as a single entity, it just multiplies the mistake to think of ourselves as a collection of smaller, single selves.

The multiplicity thesis seems most plausible when, on analysis, it is trivial. Nietzsche, for instance, wrote that the 'subject is multiplicity' and that 'we always have only a semblance of unity'.[15] But this 'always' takes the sting out of the thesis. What Nietzsche argues in *The Will to Power* is that nothing that enters consciousness is a unity. But if there are no unities, there is nothing to count, and it makes as little sense to talk about twenty personalities as it does to talk of one. It is like the difference between count nouns and non-count nouns. You can have one or two bottles of milk, but only *some* milk, not one or two milks. To say the self lacks any unity is therefore to say it is like a non-count noun, not that it is multiple. Personal identity becomes a matter of degree, of more or less, not one, two or three. On this reading, the multiplicity thesis fails because it does not take the abolition of singularity in experience far enough.

Those who stress the extent to which we are multiple are therefore more correct in what they reject than what they embrace. Even if it is too much to claim we are all plural, there is something to the idea that neither are we straightforwardly singular. Nevertheless, the singular self remains, for all its imperfections, a much better way of thinking about who we are than the hyperbolic claim that we are a multiplicity of selves. We are indeed less unified, coherent, consistent and enduring than we usually suppose, but we are still real and individual. The constructed self is robust enough to resist deconstruction from multiplicity theorists. The oneness of the self has to be understood for what it is, not rejected for what it is not.

'Each individual is part of everybody. We are all the
same mind, part of the same thing.'

Akong Tulku, Tibetan Lama

6

The social self

Sometimes we miss what is most important simply because we are looking in the wrong direction, or through the wrong end of the telescope. Could it be that our search for the self has made a fatal mistake of this kind? We been looking inwards, when perhaps all the time we should have been looking outwards. Is the key to identity to be found not in our minds, but in the social world?

The idea that the self is 'socially constructed' has been rather in vogue in some intellectual circles for some decades now. However, the idea of the 'social self' goes back to at least 1890, when William James talked about 'the images other men have framed of me' in *The Principles of Psychology*.[1] We internalise these images and they become part of our self-image. To put it simply, how we are seen by others affects how we see ourselves.

The transgender experiences of Dru Marland and Jñanamitra illustrated two ways in which this is important. First, it usually really matters to someone if there is a disconnect between how they see themselves and how others see them. This was one of the reasons Marland gave for going through the difficult process of transition. 'If you are perceived as being male, then people will treat you as a male and that is different to the way that I wanted to be treated.'

Richard Beard's book was very good at conveying the sense of how important it was for Marland to 'pass' as female. She told me that these days it's rare that she doesn't pass, and that 'the times that it does happen it tends to be with someone who wants to make a point, as in, "I can see through you", which is part of the reason why it does jar.'

A second, related way in which the social self matters is that if people are treated very differently depending on how they appear, that can change how they perceive themselves. 'I've been finding that recently I've been learning to be unconfident,' Jñanamitra told me. 'I'm now a middle-aged woman and middle-aged women in our society just disappear. So it took me really by surprise. I found myself being completely disregarded in situations. It just took my breath away really.'

Marland has had similar experiences of 'being discountenanced by men quite a lot. It's a shame that more people can't go through that at least temporarily, just to see, because unless you've seen it from one side and then the other, there's so much people take for granted. There are very few people, I think, who will behave equally to someone as male and female. The assumption is that I don't know much about anything, that my opinion is not particularly valued. Occasionally when I speak out about something I do know something about, this sense of outrage comes upon the man, usually, and the sense of wrongness that I should know about mechanics and things.'

For transgendered persons at least, the social aspect of identity is therefore of comparable importance to the bodily aspect. Hence Marland agreed when I suggested that although in a way she always had a sense of who she was, in order for that sense to be right or complete, it required physical and social changes as well. You can't just live in your private reality. What this suggests is that, like the body, the social matters primarily for how it helps frame and shape our psychological sense of self. However, some claim that this way of putting it gets things precisely the wrong way round. It is rather the case that the psychological, the inner, matters primarily for how it helps frame and shapes our social sense of self. It is our place in the world that defines who we are. The relations that constitute our identity are the relations we have with others, not those that hold between thoughts and memories in our minds. So is it true that we are social constructions?

The roles of the game

The idea that the social is important to our identity can often seem compelling once we recognise the extent to which we spend a lot of our lives in different roles. As Jacques famously put it in Shakespeare's *As You Like It*:

> All the world's a stage,
> And all the men and women merely players;
> They have their exits and their entrances,
> And one man in his time plays many parts . . .[2]

This theatrical metaphor has become the dominant means of expressing the idea that human identity is constituted by the essentially social roles we play. However, it contains within it a deep and important ambiguity. On one reading, each individual has a real self which corresponds to the identity of the actor. Like an actor, the roles we then play are not our real selves, but simply performances we put on for the sake of others. So, a man might play the roles of taxi driver, father, son, ex-husband, lover, darts team member and so on, but none of these roles reveals the real man: that lies within.

The problem with this view is that if you take away all the roles, what is left of the so-called 'real man within'? At almost every given time a man is in some kind of role, so if you strip these away, the real, inner man becomes the man only at times of solitude. This is not credible. You fully understand who a person is not by observing them in only one kind of situation, but by knowing how they are in a variety of situations. As the philosopher Janet Radcliffe Richards explains, it makes no sense to think that the real nature of something is only revealed when it is abstracted or removed from any particular environment, because everything is always in some environment or other. 'The point is,' she writes, 'that *no* single environment can show the nature of anything, because to know the nature of anything (a woman, a lump of iron, x-rays, mosquitos or black holes) is to know its *potential*; that if it is in one environment it will appear or behave in one way; that if it is in another, it may be different.'[3]

In the same way, to know a person's nature is to know how they behave in different situations, in different roles, not how they behave in one isolated role. Even if we were to believe, as we surely must, that we put on a front in some situations more than others, there is no justification for privileging solitude as the state which reveals the truth as to how we are. For one thing, it is not obvious that we play no roles when alone. Indeed, in many cases, privacy allows us to indulge the most deluded fantasies about our identities. It can be easier to convince yourself you are a rock god playing guitar in your garage than it is in front of people whose faces reveal you are no such thing. Many a person plays the role of great thinker when no one else is around to challenge their thoughts. The eyes of the world can force us to see ourselves as others see us. Alone, the image we may hold of ourselves may be no true reflection, but a flattering portrait produced by the magic mirror of vanity.

Recognising this is important for self-knowledge. We may feel most ourselves when alone, for instance, but our self-knowledge is severely limited if we fail to see how our interactions with others also reveal important truths about who we are. What we see of ourselves when we are playing no roles is not the real self, but a partial glimpse of our self.

What's more, although some people may indeed feel most fully themselves when alone, others would say the opposite. Cynics may scoff, but one of the most typical descriptions of a soul mate is someone with whom you feel completely yourself, more so than when you are alone. More typical perhaps is the extrovert who only really 'comes alive' when in company with others.

So the theatrical metaphor makes no sense if it posits the real self as the off-stage actor. The other interpretation is suggested by Jacques in *As You Like It*: that we are '*merely* players'. We are the sum of our roles, no more and no less. When you see a man in the role of a father, you are not seeing a mere performance being played by a man hiding his inner self, you are seeing one version of the real man. To extend the fiction metaphor, although the characters we play may change over time and in different situations, we only ever exist as characters. The father playing football with his son and the man lying awake in the small hours are both characters, one in a shared performance, one in a monologue.

This version of the theatrical metaphor clearly contains some truth. But its limitations are similar to those confronted by the view that we are radically multiple, which we considered in the previous chapter. The fact that we play different roles does not profoundly challenge the unity of identity, if these roles simply reflect different facets of the self. And as I argued when discussing multiplicity, in the vast majority of cases this is indeed the case. One of the quickest routes to falsehood is to overstate a truth, and this seems to me to be precisely the mistake of those who make too much of our propensity to adopt roles. That is not a mistake made by one of the seminal theoretical exponents of the theatrical metaphor, the sociologist Erving Goffman. In his book *The Presentation of Self in Everyday Life*, Goffman adopts the theatrical model as '*one* sociological perspective from which social life can be studied'.[4] The emphasis on 'one' in this sentence is mine, but it reflects accurately Goffman's claims. For instance, he talks about the 'obvious inadequacies' of the model, and having spoken 'of performers and audiences; of routines and parts; of performance coming off or falling flat', and so on, he concludes the book by saying: 'Now it should be admitted that this attempt to press an analogy so far was in part a rhetoric and a manoeuvre.'[5] It is extremely important to remember that even one of the people most responsible for popularising the idea of human life as the enacting of roles never lost sight of the fact that there were grave dangers in taking the theatrical metaphor too literally.

When you read about Goffman second-hand, however, you are often told that he thought there was no real self, only a series of performances. In fact, Goffman appears to be either agnostic about, or indifferent to, the question of the reality of different selves. His interest was not essentially *ontological*, that is to say, concerned with the nature of being. It was primarily *sociological*, concerned with the nature of social interaction. His insight is neither that the roles we play conceal our real selves nor that the roles we play are our whole selves, but that whatever we are, our interactions with others involve elements of performance that can be understood through a dramaturgical model.

One sentence in particular makes this very clear: 'While persons usually are what they appear to be, such appearances could still have been managed.' The fact that we in some sense always 'perform' when in public does not mean that we are *pretending* to be other than we really are, simply that we are controlling to some extent how the reality of who we are is presented. To switch to a cinematic metaphor, we may 'edit' and 'direct' ourselves, but it is still *ourselves* who are being edited and directed. And going back to Janet Radcliffe Richards's point, since it makes no sense to talk about presenting an unedited, undirected self, it makes no sense to think of such presentations as hiding the real self.

One reason why people overstate the importance of the social is, perhaps, that they are over-compensating for the allegedly excessive focus on inner mental life found in seminal thinkers on the self, such as Descartes. 'In their fury to be "anti-Cartesian",' writes Galen Strawson, '. . . they forget the profound and constant innerness of so much of daily experience.'[6] If you thought that our minds were self-contained units, independent of body and world, then it would be a great challenge to discover that how we think and feel depends very much on body and world. But any respectable theory will completely agree that mind is what it is because of how it is embodied and socially situated. To say that the social self matters to self-image therefore doesn't undermine the idea we keep coming back to: our identity is essentially rooted in a psychological sense of self. The fact that our minds develop in the social world, important though it is, does not change this. William James seemed to realise this. Despite emphasising the importance of the social self, he nonetheless believed that personal identity was found in the 'resemblance among the parts of a continuum of feelings' found in 'the "stream" of subjective consciousness'.[7] The social matters for the psychological, but it is still inside the mind, not outside of it, that our identity resides.

Cultural constructions

There is, however, another argument for the social construction of self, based on the claim that notions of self vary enormously from culture to culture. And on the face of it, there does seem to be a lot of evidence that this is true.

For instance, the philosopher Rom Harré has argued that the different use of personal pronouns in different cultures reflects different conceptions of the self.[8] Inuit, for example, does not have the equivalents of 'I', 'you', 's/he', 'we' and 'they'. In place of all of these are only two suffixes, '-ik' and '-tok', the former referring to the speaker, the latter referring to any other person or group of persons. Harré argues that this suggests the Eskimo sense of self is weaker than it is for us, who have many ways of self-reference, and he cites ethnographic evidence to support this view. 'Eskimo emotional states appear to be much more socially dependent than ours. Isolated Eskimos, in so far as they can be observed, seem to be stolid, neither cheerful nor depressed. But once they become part of a community (a family, say) they quickly take on the emotional tone of the community, whether they are intimately bound up with its concerns or not.' He also claims that 'all moral issues are referable only to relationships of the individual within a family group. The active, decision-making unit is not the individual human being, but the family.'

Harré is not an anthropologist and it could be that he simply has the Inuit wrong. But what if such a society did exist? It seems likely that this would be more than just a matter of holding a different *conception* of the self; the individual would *feel* differently about his or her self than a typical western European does. Self-consideration would be a very much rarer thing. A person would therefore be defined much more by their social situation than their inner consciousness.

Harré also cites the example of Japan. In Japanese, the way one refers to oneself and others always depends upon whom one is with. It is impossible to speak to anyone without the use of vocabulary indicating the social distance between you and them. This is part of a culture where much depends upon social context. In morality, for example, what is important in one area of life may not matter in another. As Harré puts it, 'The shame that diffuses that part of the psyche which has to do with others in the world of work cannot diffuse into the system within which a Japanese manages his home life.' The self, on this view, is not immutable and absolute but is something which is defined in relation to others.

However, there is clearly a danger here of exoticising the unfamiliar. The western experience of foreign cultures has always followed the pattern of first finding them utterly mysterious and 'other', only to discover in time that people are more alike in fundamentals than they are different. As the world has shrunk, belief in the inscrutable difference of other humans has not disappeared, it has just become restricted to geographically remote peoples, such as the Inuit, and selected Orientals. We should therefore be suspicious when any claim is made about other human beings which makes them fundamentally different from us.

That suspicion seems warranted in the cases Harré cites. Essentially, if his accounts are correct, social relations are much more important to the Inuit and the Japanese than they are to most Europeans. But it seems wildly implausible to leap from this to the idea that they would not, nevertheless, have the same basic sense of personal identity over time as anyone else. Indeed, the fact that the person acts and is treated differently depending on the social situation doesn't threaten the fundamental unity which underlies those diverse roles. It could be argued that without an awareness of the different roles we play, we would be unable to fulfil them properly. Although a lot of the adjustments we make to our behaviour in different contexts are unconscious, it would be very difficult, if not impossible, to make all the changes needed unless you, and others, had a sense that *you* had changed social situation.

Consider, for instance, how an Inuit would react if a person was replaced by another who slotted straight into the same social role. Of course the Inuit would both notice and consider this significant. She would also notice if the person occupying that role had a major personality change or amnesia. She would not think that because a person is defined by her social roles, the character of the individual who fulfils that role is irrelevant. That would be as implausible as a Frenchman not noticing that the President had changed after an election, because 'president' is just whoever occupies that position. We would find the contrary suggestion absurd because we simply cannot imagine what it would mean to have no sense of an individual as someone with a unique, continuing, psychological life. That could be just a failure of imagination, of course, but it seems very unlikely. Apart from anything, despite the notorious confusions of westerners trying to get by in Japanese culture, neither locals nor foreigners ever have any difficulty in treating individuals as the same individuals over time, with consistent traits, beliefs and so on. If you try to really imagine a society in which a person's own sense of their psychological continuity was not the bedrock of personal identity, I don't think you can imagine a society which is human at all.

When considering the differences between different cultures, it is important not to fall into two opposite traps. On the one hand, it is complacent to assume that everyone else is like us in all important respects. On the other, it is possible to make too much of difference and, with an over-eager desire to respect difference, to fetishise it. A good example of how to steer the middle course between this Scylla and Charybdis is the recent work of Richard E. Nisbett on the differences between how Westerners (Europeans and North Americans) and East Asians (Chinese, Japanese and Korean) think. Nisbett surveys a wide range of studies and concludes that there are real and important differences in how people from these regions tend to think. In summary form, it sounds very stereotypical. Aspects of East Asian and western thought can be lined up in diametrically opposite pairs: holistic (eastern) vs reductive (western); relational vs atomistic; community-based vs individualistic; and/both vs either/or; in flux vs rigid.

These views are not based on armchair speculations but on a number of clever experiments. In one, for instance, Japanese and American students were shown some short underwater films. When asked to describe what they had seen, both sets of students described at similar length and in similar detail the moving, foreground elements: the swimming fish. But the Japanese students made 60 per cent more reference to inert, background elements. It really does seem that they perceived their environment more holistically than the Americans, who just focused on the moving foreground.

A follow-up test seemed to confirm this. Students were shown pictures of things that had or had not featured in the film and were asked if they had seen them before. However, some were shown with their original background, whereas others were shown with a different background. This made no difference to the Americans' ability to re-identify elements correctly, but the Japanese students performed much better when shown objects with their original background. Context matters more to them.[9]

If Nisbett is correct – and there does seem to be a mountain of evidence in his favour – then we are talking about real and significant differences between the western and East Asian mind, including how westerners and easterners see themselves and others. Nevertheless, Nisbett is right not to make too much of this. It's not as though the two cultures are so far apart that people can't relate to one another. As he says, Asians have the same fundamental theories of human personality, and he could talk with Asians about 'Fung's decency and humility, Chan's arrogance, Lin's reserve, understanding each other perfectly.'[10] Also, although the differences do seem to be deeply culturally entrenched, they are far from unmalleable. Asian-Americans, for instance, display typically hybrid patterns, and Nisbett himself concludes his study by saying he expects the future to bring synthesis, not westernisation or polarisation.

Like other apparently radical attacks on the notion of a fixed self, the idea that our identities are in part culturally constructed does not leave us with good reasons to doubt that it is in the psychological unity of experience that our sense of self is to be found. Without a pearl of self, it is true that we are not as unified as we might assume, and that we are more multi-faceted. It is also true that the social roles we play, and the cultures that we live in, may fashion our senses of who we are. But none of this should shake our belief that our unity as individuals is rooted in a psychological sense of self, and that this unity is real, if not absolute.

So far, all roads have led us back to this psychological sense of self. However, I have not yet presented a positive account of what that unity really amounts to. It's time, finally, to set out what it is that really makes us who we are.

'I wouldn't expect acceptance of "the true view" to have great transformative powers, chiefly because the true view is so hard to accept.'

Derek Parfit, philosopher

7

The Ego Trick

Before giving a full account of what the correct view of the self is, let's first sum up where we've got to. My argument so far supports four main claims:

First, there is no thing or part of you which contains your essence. Your body, your brain and your memories are all very important for who you are, but none of these is the pearl of self in which your identity resides.

Second, you have no immaterial soul. Whatever stuff you are made from, it is the same kind of stuff that everything else is made of, be it plankton, cabbages or orang-utans.

Third, given that the pearl view is to be rejected, this means that your sense of self must in some way be a construction. If there is no single thing which makes you the person you are, then you must be the result of several parts or things working together.

Fourth, the unity which enables you to think of yourself as the same person over time is in some ways fragile, and in others robust. So although we may not be unified in the simple, strong way the pearl view suggests, that does not mean that we go wrong when we think of ourselves as integrated individuals. We may be more internally fragmented than common sense assumes, but that does not mean we are radically multiple, and should give up thinking of ourselves in the first-person singular. Our sense of self may well be strongly affected by the social world we inhabit, but the sense itself remains inner, psychological.

If I've done my job, then these claims should seem to be not just true, but perhaps even obvious. But the truth often seems obvious in retrospect. It is easy to forget how each one of these claims has not generally been a part of received wisdom, nor informed wisdom, for that matter.

However, by themselves, these truths leave a lot of unanswered questions and problems. Together, they tell us we are *unified, material constructions*. Each one of these words is problematic. The degree to which we are *unified* is still vague. We say we are in some sense *constructions*, but it is not clear how we are put together. We know that bodies, memories and society all play a role, but how does a strong sense of self emerge from their interaction? And the extent to which we are *material* is also puzzling, given that our mental life gives us the strongest sense of who we are, not our bodies. That is why transgendered people can know who they are even when their bodies are wrong or change, and why we often feel loved ones with dementia have left us, even as their diseased bodies continue to live.

In this chapter, I'm going to try to answer these questions and flesh out what I think the correct view of our selves should be. I will be building on and synthesising arguments given by a string of major thinkers in eastern and western traditions. To do this, there is no avoiding the introduction of some technical conceptual distinctions, but although this chapter may require closer reading than those that have preceded it, there is nothing here that assumes specialised prior knowledge.

My case will rest on three main claims, the first of which will probably seem obvious, the second perhaps surprising, and the third potentially outrageous. This an argumentative trajectory with a good philosophical pedigree. 'The point of philosophy,' wrote Bertrand Russell, 'is to start with something so simple as not to seem worth stating, and to end with something so paradoxical that no one will believe it.'[1]

1. The unity of the self is psychological

I've already mentioned John Locke's definition of a person as a 'thinking intelligent being that has reflection and can consider itself as itself, the same thinking thing in different times and places'. Did he, I wonder, think this was a statement of the obvious? That might be putting it too strongly, but it is clear that Locke was offering a definition he believed most people would, on reflection, readily accept. If it wasn't entirely self-evident, it should not have been controversial either.

In my experience, most people respond to Locke's definition with a shoulder-shrug, as though it really doesn't tell us anything we don't already know. But it is in the unpacking of the idea that we see its full implications, and recognise that it is not harmlessly banal after all. Consider, for instance, what Locke has to say about the immaterial soul. He doesn't bother arguing that it doesn't exist, because he doesn't need to. On his view of persons, souls are irrelevant:

> Let any one reflect upon himself, and conclude that he has in himself an immaterial spirit, which is that which thinks in him, and, in the constant change of his body keeps him the same: and

is that which he calls himself. Let him also suppose it to be the same soul that was in Nestor or Thersites, at the siege of Troy (for souls being, as far as we know anything of them, in their nature indifferent to any parcel of matter, the supposition has no apparent absurdity in it), which it may have been, as well as it is now the soul of any other man: but he now having no consciousness of any of the actions either of Nestor or Thersites, does or can he conceive himself the same person with either of them? Can he be concerned in either of their actions? attribute them to himself, or think them his own, more than the actions of any other men that ever existed?[2]

The questions are rhetorical. Locke continues, 'He is no more one self with either of them than if the soul or immaterial spirit that now informs him had been created, and began to exist, when it began to inform his present body.' In itself, having the soul of someone now dead no more makes you that person than having the same liver would. Souls would only preserve identity if they took their consciousness with them.

Locke's point is so self-evident that you can't even call it an argument. Just asking the right questions, ones which make us attend to the right things, is enough to show that there is something deeply wrong with the idea that the continuity of some non-physical part itself ensures the continuity of the person. We *observe* that Locke is right, we do not *deduce* that he is.

The radical import of Locke's idea is made even clearer when you consider that it makes possible non-human persons. On Locke's definition, any animal, or alien, would be a person, just as long as it was a 'thinking intelligent being that has reflection and can consider itself as itself, the same thinking thing in different times and places'. It is on grounds like these that some people argue that there are indeed some non-human persons. The bioethicist Peter Singer has argued that 'some nonhuman animals are persons', most notably chimpanzees and bonobos.[3] That view is shared by many other supporters of The Great Ape Project, which aims to confer several hitherto exclusively human rights to chimpanzees, gorillas, orang-utans and bonobos. Similarly, ethicist Thomas I. White has argued for granting the status of personhood to dolphins.[4]

While many see such claims to be excessive, it is surely not because the principle behind them is wrong. That principle is that 'person' is not a *biological* category, but a *functional* one. Any creature, or even machine, that has the conscious capacities of a person is a person, irrespective of its species. That is why we recognise as *people* characters in science-fiction films who are human-like but of another species. Were we to be visited by any such friendly aliens, we would surely treat them as persons, not animals. Similarly, if a parrot could discourse as lucidly and coherently as a person, then we would consider it to be a fully formed person, not just a bird.

What makes for a single person over time is therefore, in the formulation of contemporary philosopher Derek Parfit, *psychological connectedness and continuity*. That is why a person remains the same person, even when their bodies radically change. That is why we doubt whether the person we once knew still exists when the continuity has been severely disrupted by disease or brain trauma. That is why memory seems intuitively to be so important to personal identity, but is not enough to fix it, because it is the primary but not only source of psychological connectedness and continuity. It is also why brains matter so much for identity, but again do not define it, because functioning brains are the only means we have of creating and sustaining psychological unity, but the mere continued existence of a brain does not guarantee it. And it is also why the bodies we have and the role we play in society are important but not defining aspects of self, since both help fashion our psychological sense of self without completely determining it.

Again, if this all sounds obvious, it is probably because some of the more radical implications are being missed. Perhaps most importantly, we need to remember that on this view, persons are constructions. Psychological connectedness and continuity is not the result of any core pearl of self that carries the continuity. Rather, this is sometimes called a 'bundle theory'. The eighteenth-century philosopher David Hume was the first to use 'bundle' in this context, just once. His contemporary Thomas Reid picked up on it, attributing to Hume the view that 'what we call the mind, is only a bundle of thoughts, passions, and emotions, without any subject'.[5] Like many descriptions which start out as mockery, the term has stuck. To see what this means, put this book aside for a moment, introspect and try to find the you that has all the thoughts, memories and so on.

Did you succeed? If so, you had more joy than David Hume, godfather of bundle theorists, who wrote: 'For my part, when I enter most intimately into what I call *myself*, I always stumble on some particular perception or other, of heat or cold, light or shade, love or hatred, pain or pleasure, colour or sound, etc. I never catch *myself*, distinct from some such perception.' Our minds are just one perception or thought after another, one piled on another. You, the person, is not separate from these thoughts, the thing having them. Rather you just are the collection of these thoughts, 'nothing but a bundle or collection of different perceptions, which succeed each other with an inconceivable rapidity, and are in a perpetual flux and movement'.[6]

This is the heart of the Ego Trick. The trick is to create something which has a strong sense of unity and singleness from what is actually a messy, fragmented sequence of experiences and memories, in a brain which has no control centre. The point is that *the trick works*. It's like a mechanic's trick, not a magician's trick. The magician's aim is to get you to believe that something has happened which never did. The tricks of mechanics, engineers and scientists, in contrast, are short cuts or improvisations that enable them to get systems to behave as they want them to behave, bypassing the usual means of doing so. So if your car needs a repair and the mechanic can't get the part, he might have a 'trick' that gets the car working as normal anyway.

The Ego Trick should be seen in this way. There is no single thing which comprises the self, but we need to function as though there were. As it happens, the mind, thanks to the brain and body, has all sorts of tricks up its sleeve that enable us to do this. Because it succeeds, selves really do exist. We only go wrong if we're too impressed by this unity and assume that it means that underlying it is a single thing. But the self is not a substance or thing, it is a function of what a certain collection of stuff does.

I'll be saying more about how and why the bundle theory is true in the rest of this chapter. But if it does seem a strange, implausible idea, it's worth remembering just how much of reality is bundle-like. Atoms are not solid objects but bundles of electrons, neutrons and protons. A plant is a complicated system, not a simple thing. Cars only exist as an assemblage of parts. The internet is a network, not an object that can pinned down in time and space. If it seems odd to think of ourselves as 'bundles' then perhaps that is only because we do not notice the extent to which all other entities are bundles too.

The systematic elusiveness of 'I'

I'm sure some readers will suspect me of making too quick a leap in the last section. I'd imagine that most people would be happy to accept that psychological continuity is the key to personal identity. But was the move from that to bundles too swift? Go back to Hume's introspective findings. You might think that there is a sleight of hand going on here. Sure, you probably did not come across a perception of yourself when you turned your gaze inwards, but perhaps that should not be surprising. We do not observe the self in the same way that we observe the yellowness of a tulip, the smell of coffee or the thought that I really must book my train. The self is what is *having* those thoughts and perceptions – it is not itself a perception. And when you introspect, you might argue, you *are* always aware that there is a self having thoughts and perceptions. If not, there could be no awareness at all.

To put it another way, what Gilbert Ryle calls the 'systematic elusiveness of "I"'[7] is simply a result of the impossibility of being both subject and object at the same time. The 'I' cannot catch itself for the same kind of reason that a hunter cannot be its own prey. It would be like trying to eat your own face, or look directly into your own eyes (without the aid of a reflection, of course). In that sense, 'I' is elusive in the same way that 'now' is. As soon as you have tried to refer to the present moment, it has passed. Likewise, when you try to observe your own self, to become fully self-conscious, that very act changes the nature of the experience you are trying to observe.

There is an important insight here. Those who try to reduce a self to bundles have to be able to account for what the philosopher Paul Ricoeur called 'the tenacity of personal pronouns'.[8] You cannot even say 'I am a bundle' without using a word – I – that seems to refer to a single, unitary thing. The contemporary philosopher Quassim Cassam goes further, arguing that it is not possible 'to capture the content of an I-thought without ascribing it to a person or subject',[9] and that self-consciousness itself requires that 'we are aware of ourselves as abiding material substances, as physical objects among physical objects'.[10]

Cassam follows in the footsteps of Immanuel Kant, who argued that for experience of the world to be possible, there has to be a fundamental unity within the subject of experience which allows the world to be perceived. Kant calls this the 'transcendental unity of apperception': the unity of inner experience necessary for any particular experience of the world to be perceived as part of a wider, unified whole. There must be an 'I think' which necessarily accompanies all thought, which allows the manifold of experiences to be grasped as a coherent whole in conscious experience.

These arguments seem compelling, but attempts to work out from the armchair what is necessary for experience to be possible, as Cassam and Kant do, are always vulnerable to facts emerging on the ground which plain contradict them. People with Cotard Syndrome or transient epileptic amnesia, for instance, which we came across in Chapter Two, simply do not conform to Cassam's armchair stipulations about what is necessary for coherent, conscious experience of the world. Also, Antti Revonsuo's survey of research into dreaming suggests that it is not uncommon to find that there is no self present in the dream at all.[11] If this is right, then it falsifies Kant's claim that there can be no unity of apperception without an I. Likewise, in dreams we are sometimes disembodied, contradicting Cassam's claim that in order to be conscious, we have to be aware of ourselves as abiding material substances.

We have to be very careful what conclusions we draw from the alleged necessity of thinking of ourselves as singular, unified entities. It may indeed be necessary for me to think of myself as an embodied subject, for example, but that does not show that I *am* necessarily an embodied subject at all times. I may have to think of myself as having a unity over time, but that does not mean that I really have it. How *we must think* about things at certain times, for certain purposes, in certain ways, does not necessarily tells us about how *they actually are*. Kant recognised this: 'The identity of the consciousness of myself at different times is therefore only a formal condition of my thoughts and their coherence, and in no way proves the numerical identity of my subject.'[12] Or, in Galen Strawson's words, 'self-experience exists, as a form of experience, whether or not selves do'.[13]

The unity of experience does not therefore demonstrate that there is a unified thing having those experiences. Indeed, the evidence is that there is no such thing. There is no place in the brain where it all comes together and there is no immaterial soul which is the seat of consciousness. The unity we experience, which allows us legitimately to talk of 'I', is a result of the Ego Trick – the remarkable way in which a complicated bundle of mental events, made possible by the brain, creates a singular self, without there being a singular *thing* underlying it. It seems as though there is some pearl at the self's core, but in fact there is no core at all. Generations of thinkers have gone wrong in thinking that we need to postulate a unified core self to account for the unity of self-experience. In fact, unity is not a cause: it is an effect of a remarkably disunified, bundle-like system.

2. We are no more than, but more than just, matter

But isn't there still something not right about the view I've been putting forward? On the one hand, I've been arguing that we are entirely physical, and that we have no material souls. But on the other, I insist we are not our brains or our bodies, and that our identity is defined by psychological continuity. We seem to be wholly physical yet oddly not essentially physical at all.

The key to understanding how this can be so lies in a proper understanding of what it is to say that we are biological creatures. Again, we have to be wary of the debunking 'mere' or 'just'. Even those who in their materialist zeal say that we are no more than cells and bodies do not generally deny the obvious fact that these cells and bodies have thoughts, feelings, relationships, dreams, desires and so on. The way I put it is that *we are no more than, but more than just, matter*. In other words, we are made up of nothing more than physical stuff, but to describe our true nature, you need more than just a physical vocabulary. You cannot fully describe what it is to be a person in the language of biology; but that does not mean a person has non-biological parts.

This way of looking at things – sometimes called non-reductive physicalism – seems to be the only way to reconcile three seemingly obvious truths. The first is that thoughts, feelings, emotions and so on are real. There are some 'eliminative materialists' who claim that they aren't, but in I.A. Richards's famous phrase, such thinkers seem to 'feign anaesthesia', claiming not to have experiences which surely they do.

The second truth is that whatever thoughts and feelings are, they are not straightforwardly physical. You can't see a memory under a microscope, and an emotion has no mass or velocity. It is true that with fMRI scanners you can see the brain activity *associated* with such experiences, and perhaps in the future we will be able to say exactly what the experience is purely on the basis of such observations. But no matter how good the technology gets, there is always a difference between observing a brain event and experiencing a mental event. To use the jargon, we can see the 'neural correlates of consciousness', but that does not make us conscious of what it is a correlate of. I can observe your brain listening to music, but that is not the same as hearing it myself.

To these we can add the third truth: that there is no stuff in the universe other than the stuff of physics. Not so long ago, you could have put that same basic thought in simpler terms and it would probably have been more persuasive: there is nothing in the universe apart from matter. That formulation has become both less persuasive and less accurate, since developments in physics have changed the way we think about the fundamental constituents of the universe. The best simplification we can now come up with is that the universe is at root comprised of energy, but at the smallest, quantum level, this energy is so weird and mysterious it's difficult to know how to describe it in ways that aren't contentious and question-begging.

But if it is too simplistic to say that atoms are all that there is, the view that we just have no idea what there is, is too pessimistic. The mysteries of quantum physics have unfortunately become a cover for all sorts of unwarranted speculations, providing a pseudo-scientific veneer for what has no basis in fact. For instance, I have heard a theologian argue that since 95 per cent of the universe is made up of dark matter, and we have no idea what this dark matter is, we have no basis for claiming that anything, including human beings, is no more than matter.

This is misguided, because it fails to take account of the extent to which the only way physicists can really understand the universe is in the language of mathematics. The fundamental basis of physics is not atoms, or even subatomic particles, but equations. That is why, for all its mysteriousness, dark matter does have all the reality that is needed for physics: it plugs into the equations. Indeed, it is because the equations make it necessary that the existence of dark matter was postulated before it could be detected. So, odd though it may sound, the best definition of the physical world we now have is 'that which has a place in the equations of physicists'. And one thing you can say with certainty about souls is that they have no place there.

So we have these three facts: thoughts and feelings are real, they are not describable in purely physical terms, but the universe has within it only the physical things described by the equations of physicists. It seems the only way to make sense of this is that mental events *emerge* from physical ones, without being strictly identical with them. As the neurologist Todd E. Feinberg puts it, 'your life is not a pack of cells; your life is what your particular pack of cells collectively do, though I cannot observe such a thing as your life, touch it, put it under a microscope, or keep it in a bottle on shelf.'[14] Thought and feeling are what matter *does*, when it is arranged in the remarkably complex ways that brains are. Matter is all that is needed for them to exist, but they are not themselves lumps of matter. In this sense, 'I' is a verb dressed as a noun.

The idea that the mental emerges from the physical is a tricky one. It looks to me like a partial description masquerading as an explanation. What I mean is, to say consciousness is an emergent property is not to explain consciousness at all. To do that you'd have to explain *how* it emerges, and although some claim to have done that, most remain unconvinced. But what does seem to be true is that consciousness does indeed emerge from complex physical events in the brain, even if we don't know *how* it does so. Whatever the mechanism, we have thoughts and feelings because we have physical brains that work, not because there's something else in our heads doing the mental work instead. The evidence for this is simple but overwhelming: damage the brain, and you impair consciousness. Change the chemicals in the brain, and you change consciousness. Stimulate certain parts of the brain, and you get a certain kind of experience. To accept this (as surely we must) but insist that brains aren't the engines of thought is not impossible, but it is perverse.

This helps us to explain more fully how the Ego Trick works. It is able to create something which has a strong sense of unity and singleness from what is actually a messy, fragmented sequence of experiences and memories, because all mental experience emerges from a messy, fragmented and hugely complicated set of processes in the brain. We do not yet fully understand how this trick works, but we know that it does. Those who hold on to the idea that something other than a functioning brain is required to create persons with a sense of self are simply not looking the evidence in the face. Just because some mysteries remain, that does not mean that everything is a mystery, and it certainly doesn't mean we are justified in appealing to other mysteries, like souls, to plug the gaps in our understanding. On the question of whether we are physical beings or not, the case should be closed.

Body matters

It is important to stress the physical basis of personhood in order to answer critics who argue that the contemporary philosophy of personal identity suffers from the same disability that has plagued western philosophy since its inception: it is so centred on rational thought that it either downplays or ignores the importance of our less rational features. The most significant victim of this 'ratio-centrism' is the body. And if you want to know why the intellectual crime has been committed, maybe a clue is in the canon of great philosophers: they're all male. 'From the beginnings of philosophical thought,' writes the philosopher Genevieve Lloyd, 'femaleness was symbolically associated with what reason left behind.'[15] In western culture, mind and reason are 'coded' masculine, while emotion and body are coded feminine. Men are ruled by their heads, women by their hearts. Although this coding has traditionally been used to mark the male as superior, it is also adopted by some difference feminists, who celebrate the 'earth mother' precisely for having a deeper connection with body and feeling than the now excessively rational male.

One example of this phallocentric bias is evident in a popular thought experiment. Imagine your mind being transferred to another body, either by a brain transplant or by 'reprogramming'. Susan James is one of several philosophers to have pointed out that the intelligibility of such thought experiments becomes more problematic if you imagine being given a new body which is of a different gender. Most of the leading (male) thought experimenters, however, simply gloss over this problem, she says. Bernard Williams notes the difficulty but says 'let us forget this' while Harold Noonan simply specifies that, for the sake of the thought experiment, the bodies should be thought of as qualitatively the same or at least very similar.[16]

The logical consequence of this ratiocentrism – whether it is the result of male dominance or not – was the pure intellect of Descartes' *cogito*: the 'I think' which contains our essence. If reason defines our highest, truest selves, and bodies are simply a necessary, perhaps temporary inconvenience, then the philosopher who asks 'what am I?' is sure to conclude that he is in essence pure mind, untainted by matter. But as the psychiatrist R.D. Laing points out, 'a divorce of self from body' is the mark of psychosis, not deep philosophical insight, at least when it becomes a matter of how you experience yourself rather than simply theorise it. It is pathological when 'the body is felt more as one object among other objects in the world than as the core of the individual's own being'.[17]

Of course, a philosopher of Descartes' undoubted genius is not going to completely miss the fact that this ego is very much embodied. In a passage often quoted by those seeking to defend Descartes against the charge of ignoring the body, he writes: 'Nature also teaches me, by these sensations of pain, hunger, thirst and so on, that I am not merely present in my body as a sailor is present in a ship, but that I am very closely joined and, as it were, intermingled with it, so that I and the body form a unit.'[18] But what Descartes admits in this sentence he simultaneously takes back, for the psychosomatic unit he describes is nonetheless a combination of 'I' and 'body'. He may be *intermingled* with a body, but the body is not *him*. As he puts it in the very next sentence, 'I, who am nothing but a thinking thing'.

As we have seen, there are very few hard-nosed Cartesians knocking about these days, but it is often argued that Cartesian assumptions are to be found lurking behind numerous officially non-dualistic theories. Such an accusation is made against contemporary bundle theorists, who have no time for non-material souls but whose emphasis on psychological continuity as the key to personal identity is allegedly Cartesian through and through. Mind and body are not cleaved as distinct *substances*, but their separation as *properties* is nonetheless just as binary as it was in Descartes. Properties of mind define who we are, properties of body are simply relegated to the necessary material substrate.

The legacy of Descartes has also come under attack in neuroscience, explicitly so in the case of Antonio Damasio, who called one of his books *Descartes' Error*. Damasio's target is not just the general separation of mind and body, but the distinction between reason and emotion which it is deeply connected to. Damasio's general hypothesis is that emotions are in fact essential to rational decision-making. Reason and emotion therefore can't be separated, because the proper operation of the former requires and involves the latter: 'Well-targeted and well-deployed emotion seems to be a support system without which the edifice of reason cannot operate properly.'[19] What's more, emotions are not produced simply in the brain. Rather, 'the body is the main stage for emotions, either directly or via its representation in somatosensory structures of the brain.' This is because 'feelings are largely a reflection of body-state changes'.[20]

Although I think it is true that bundle theories have not given due attention to the importance of our bodies, this is not a fatal flaw, but an easily corrected oversight. The key to rectifying the error is to have a richer understanding of what the psychological really is, and with it what 'psychological continuity' really means. There is nothing about the very concept of the psychological that requires us to think of it as being separate or separable from the physical. That is why we can make perfect sense of thinkers like Damasio when they insist that the psychological is intimately connected with the somatic.

Descartes' error was to think that mind and body are of different orders, not that mind exists.

You only have to consider the scope of what we would call the 'mental' in ordinary speech to see that it would be a very peculiar use of the word to think of it as only involving *conscious, rational thoughts*. To take the middle term first, it is quite obvious that many of our thoughts are far from rational. What's more, the mental includes much more than thought. Our mental world is also populated by sensations; emotions; the words, tunes and images that flit around our heads; dreams; desires and so on. Many, if not all, of these are intimately linked with our bodies. So if it is understood coherently, the very notion of psychological continuity assumes a large degree of physical continuity, because a great deal of what fills our minds is intimately tied up with our bodies.

It's also worth saying something at this point about the role of the unconscious. Many of a psychoanalytic bent also criticise the kind of analytic, philosophical account of personal identity I have presented for neglecting that of which we are not conscious. It would indeed be wrong to limit the psychological to conscious experience. There are unconscious drivers of our mental lives which are integral to their operation. Psychological continuity therefore requires some continuity in what is unconscious too. But it is important to realise that this is so only because the conscious cannot be the way it is without the unconscious. The unconscious matters because of its influence on the conscious, not in its own right.

To see why, we simply have to ask what it means to say a person has, for instance, a subconscious desire for fame. To say it is subconscious means that the person is *not aware of the effect* the desire is having on his conscious life. It does not mean that *it has no effect*. Indeed, it is difficult to see what the latter would even mean. If an unconscious desire makes no difference to anything in conscious life, then it is at best redundant: it would make no difference at all whether it existed or not. It would not be required for psychological continuity, because a person's life would continue identically whether this mysterious unconscious desire existed or not.

Both our bodies and our unconscious desires, beliefs and so forth therefore matter to psychological continuity to the extent to which they shape conscious life. Combine this with the acceptance that a lot of conscious experience is directly related to the body and you can see how a proper understanding of psychological continuity *assumes* an important role for the body, rather than denies it. Any bundle theorists who did ignore the body would therefore really be ignoring important aspects of the mind. Psychological continuity, properly understood, pays due homage to our physicality.

3. Identity is not what matters

It is time to confess that in defending the idea that psychological continuity is the basis of our identity over time, I've so far been a little disingenuous. The problem comes with the word 'identity'. The truth is, I've been using the term somewhat loosely. Try to tighten it up, however, and it cracks. That's because, strictly speaking, 'identity' is the wrong concept to apply to persons. To explain why, it's necessary to go into a little bit of logical analysis.

For philosophers, 'identity' comes in two main forms: *quantitative* and *qualitative*. Two or more things are qualitatively identical when interchanging them would make no difference. For instance, if you have two qualitatively identical bowling balls, it makes no difference which one you pick up when you attempt a strike.

Such qualitatively identical objects, however, are not quantitatively the same: they are not literally the same object. If you put a mark on one of the balls, the other is unaffected. If you smash one, you do not smash the other. If one is in one place, the other can't be literally in the same place too. When we talk about the identity of objects over time, it is this quantitative identity that we are interested in. We want to know if the very same object has persisted over time, not merely whether two objects at different times are indistinguishable.

Quantitative identity is governed by a strict logic, summed up in what has become known as Leibniz's law. In essence this says that if x and y are the same object, then what is true of x at any given time is also true of y at that same time. This is why two merely qualitatively identical bowling balls are not the same ball. If it is true of the first that it is on top of the second, then it cannot also be true of the second that it is on top of the first. If, however, I am told that ball x has the same size, weight, colour, composition and location as ball y, at the same time, then I know ball x is ball y. It's the same logic that enables you to know that if Colonel Mustard was in the same room as the murderer, and that the only people in the room were the murderer and the victim, and that Colonel Mustard is not the victim, then Colonel Mustard is the murderer. The logic is unavoidable.

The problem is that this logically strict notion of sameness only works for reasonably solid, stable objects. In all sorts of real-world cases, notions of 'sameness' are vaguer and more context-dependent. Take Hobbes's famous example of the ship of Theseus.[21] This vessel is taken into dry dock for repairs. The masts are broken, so these are replaced. The hull is rotting, so that too is rebuilt with new timber. Then it's noticed the deck is looking a bit worn, so that too is replaced. And so on, until no parts of the ship are the same as when it came in. So is it the same ship? And what if someone took all the old bits and put them back together? Would that have a stronger claim to being the original ship of Theseus?

The obvious answer is that it depends. There isn't really a single fact of the matter. As long as you know what aspect of sameness matters to the questioner, you can provide an answer. If you're a forensic investigator searching for traces of DNA left before the ship went into dock, the boat you want is the one rebuilt from original parts. If you're Theseus, your ship is the totally renovated one. If you know what aspect of sameness matters, you can provide a clear answer. What you can't do is answer the general question, 'but which one is really the same ship?' It's an *empty question*: it looks like a genuine question that should have an answer, but it has none.

All sorts of questions of sameness in real life are of this kind. For instance, I went to a fortieth anniversary concert by the rock band Hawkwind. But was it really the *same* Hawkwind that formed in 1969? There is no simple factual answer. But you don't need one: I can tell you all the important facts. There has been a band called Hawkwind working continuously since 1969, various members have come and gone, but one of the founding members has been there throughout. If I explain all this and you still insist, 'But is it the same band?' you're asking an empty question.

Although in some ways philosophers are fond of the answer 'It depends', they can't stand it when what it depends on can't be rigorously formalised. They hate vagueness, to the point of being *incertophobic*. But although it is right to despise being vague about what could be more precise, it is wrong to try to be too precise about what is of its nature vague. Similarly, philosophers do not like to rely too much on personal judgements. But again, although it is wrong to rely on a subjective judgement if an objective one can be made, it is just as wrong to try to avoid subjective judgements when they are unavoidable.

I think we have seen numerous cases where it should be obvious that strict logical identity is the wrong way to think about persons. Take the strange case of brain-hemisphere transplant discussed by Richard Swinburne, where a brain is divided and is put into two bodies, both of which continue the consciousness of the person with the original, single brain. Don't worry about whether this is actually possible (it almost certainly isn't). The question is, *if* we could do this to me, would I be the same person as Rightian, Leftian, none or both? In the strict logical sense, most would say the answer has to be none. But in the existential sense, surely the sense that really matters here, the answer is, it depends. In some ways you are, in some ways you're not. As with the ship of Theseus, the important question is not about identity but about *what matters*.

The same is true when we talk about people in the late stages of dementia. Are they they same persons we knew before the disease took its hold? In some ways yes, in some ways no. It depends. To expect the logic of identity to yield a clear answer is foolish.

One way of looking at this is that, rather than there being one question of personal identity, there are actually (at least) two different questions. There is a *logical* question about the identity of objects and the *existential* question about what matters to us about our survival and the survival of those we care about. In that sense, animalism – the idea we started Chapter One with, that our identity is a matter of being a particular biological animal – could be the right answer to the wrong question. It could be that the only way to specify the logical identity of the things we are over time is to think of ourselves as biological animals. But even if that is true, it leaves untouched the existential question that really matters to us, the question of how I should think about and relate to past and future versions of me.

Unfortunately, most philosophers of personal identity have been caught in the spell of 'identity' and, as a result, their arguments have gone badly wrong. And when philosophy goes wrong, it's like watching people try to nail custard to the wall. Worse, they just won't stop their hammering, insisting that if custard is a real thing, which surely it is, then it should be possible to pin it down. The root of the problem is that philosophy's deep and deserved respect for the combined might of language and logic often becomes an unhealthy reverence.

It is not enough that words and reason are extremely powerful, they have to be supremely powerful. What they can't master isn't worth mastering.

Not all philosophers have suffered from this misapprehension, of course. The best, to my mind, are precisely those who manage both to be no less precise than necessary, but no more precise than is possible. Paul Ricoeur is a rare example of a philosopher who seems to appreciate the unsuitability of applying logical identity to persons. His central idea is captured in the phrase 'selfhood is not sameness'.[22] Ricoeur uses the Latin terms *idem* and *ipse* to distinguish between sameness and selfhood. Sameness, *idem*, is unique and recurrent: one thing continuing to exist as exactly the same thing over time. In other words, *idem* is what we have called quantitative identity. But selves do not have this sameness over time. It is in their nature to change, never exactly the same from one day to the next. The trouble is that we tend to use the word 'identity' in relation to persons, unclear as to whether we mean sameness (*idem*) or selfhood (*ipse*). What we need to be clear about is that persons retain a sense of selfhood over time, but this is not a precise sameness.

Ludwig Wittgenstein is another thinker who can help explain why exactitude is not always possible. He saw that many words and concepts do not have precise rules for their use, and cannot have their meanings analysed in strict logical terms. Wittgenstein famously used the example of 'game'. What is the precise definition of a game? Games are so varied that it is impossible to specify them without there being exceptions. Games are usually for fun, but war games aren't, nor are all the games people play in relationships. Many games have winners and losers, but many playground games, for instance, are just fun activities.

Wittgenstein argued that meanings of words often cannot be specified in logically comprehensive terms. 'For a *large* class of cases – though not for all – in which we employ the word "meaning" it can be defined thus: the meaning of a word is its use in the language.'[23] (Ironically, this is often quoted without the initial qualification, making the definition appear to apply to all meaning. Wittgenstein's defence of vagueness is thus more precise than is often believed.) In other words, to understand a word, sometimes you can do no better than learn by experience how it is used in different contexts. Everyone is familiar, I think, with the realisation that our competence to use a word accurately often exceeds our ability to define it precisely. Wittgenstein's insight is that this is not paradoxical, but a reflection of the true nature of meaning itself.

Wittgenstein knew that other philosophers would not like this dangerous descent into vagueness. 'But is a blurred concept a concept at all?' he imagined them objecting. 'Is an indistinct photograph a picture of a person at all?' he answered. 'Is it even always an advantage to replace an indistinct picture by a sharp one? Isn't the indistinct one often exactly what we need?'[24]

Fuzziness is not only a matter of concepts but of things. Custard cannot be nailed to a wall, not because the word 'custard' is vague, but because the sauce itself is not solid enough. Likewise, there are many things that really exist, but whose natures are indistinct. Love is one example. Most obviously, the fact that it is not an object with mass, length and depth does not mean it is not real. More significantly perhaps, our inability to define it precisely is not a limitation of language but a reflection of the fact that its nature is not precisely bounded.

Most non-philosophers have little trouble accepting that both language and the world are full of fuzzy borders. But much philosophy is actually done as though this were not obvious at all. The philosophy of personal identity is, unfortunately, a prime example of this. It is fatally flawed by its goal of stating the strict logical conditions for the persistence of a person over time. Because this is how the whole debate is framed, it tends to underestimate the reality and significance of the vagueness inherent both in the concepts surrounding persons and in persons themselves. The theories thus say more about the logic of the concepts they employ than the phenomena they describe. And because many of the most important aspects of being a person do not yield to precise analysis, the precise answers philosophers then give end up being based on those that do, whether they are the most important or not. The quest for precision makes them take their eye off the fuzzy ball.

The false assumption can be put in another way. Concepts such as 'person' and 'self' are taken to be either 'sortals' or useless. A sortal concept is one which allows you to count the number of things to which that concept applies, and to specify the conditions for their identity at a time and over time. The distinction is similar to the grammatical one between count nouns and mass nouns, so 'love' and 'water' are not sortals, but 'computer' and 'ball' are. Given this distinction, isn't it obvious that 'person' and 'self' must be sortal concepts?

Most philosophers of personal identity accept this. But I think the animalists are right to say that, given this assumption, theirs becomes the only coherent view, because nothing else other than the human animal is sufficiently well defined and definable to stand up as a candidate for a persisting entity over time. Bundles of thoughts and feelings are too amorphous to yield to the logic of identity. Some, like Thomas Nagel, have argued that the brain does the job well enough, but brains do not exist in isolation from whole bodies. They may indeed be the most important part of ourselves, but to identify a whole with what is simply one of its parts, no matter how important, is to commit what Max Bennett and Peter Hacker call the 'mereological fallacy'.[25] What's more, brains can be split, in theory if not in practice.

So if you really do want to reject animalism, it may be necessary to follow a route marked out but not recommended by Harold

Noonan and 'accept that the concept of person is not a sortal concept at all'. Lest the seriousness of this move not be appreciated, Noonan points out that to do so would involve 'the radical claim that the topic of personal identity is strictly speaking non-existent'.[26]

Few are happy to go down this road. For instance, I put it to Derek Parfit that 'in effect we have two (sets of) philosophical questions: one about personal identity and one about what matters in survival. They are not unrelated, of course, but it does mean that it is more than possible that arguments about personal identity may have nothing to do with what matters in survival.' He replied: 'In a way, I agree. But since most people will continue to believe, or be very strongly inclined to believe, that personal identity is what matters, we shall need to discuss this question. And even on a view like mine, personal identity is fairly closely correlated with what matters.'[27]

I don't think it aids the cause of clarity to continue to focus on something closely correlated, but not identical to, the issue that matters, rather than the issue itself. Nor should what most people think determine what we choose as our primary issue. So I'm happy to bite both Noonan's bullets. In fact, I chew them with relish. 'Person' is not best thought of as a robust sortal concept and so 'personal identity' is strictly speaking non-existent.

The idea that 'person' is not a sortal concept may seem bizarre. How could we possibly have a concept of person that did not allow us to count how many there are in the room? But this only seems radical if one assumes that the choice is between a strict sortal and a totally vague mass noun. This is just another false dichotomy created by putting logic first and the reality of language and the world second. Person is not a sortal *in the strict sense* for reasons that should by now be obvious. The boundaries of the self are not precise, and there may be times, real and imaginary, when it really is not possible to say how many there are or whether they are identical with past or future selves. But for practical purposes we can usually say how many persons are in a room, or whether I am the same person as I was yesterday.

The distinction I am making here is between strict logical identity and what we might call *pragmatic* identity. There are numerous examples of words and concepts that are not strict sortals yet which can usually be used as though they were. Take the act of 'having sex'. I'm always a little puzzled by the ease with which people will report how many times they had sex over a given timescale. How exactly do they count? We don't normally ask the question because we assume we know what is meant. But try to specify it and you can see it is actually not unambiguous. Some (men, mainly) will take it to mean the number of times they achieved orgasm. But would they say they didn't have sex if they made love and didn't climax? And what if between orgasms the lovemaking didn't stop? Did the woman, or the man, have sex twice or once? It should be pretty obvious both that there is no right answer and that, for practical purposes, it usually doesn't matter. 'Having sex' is not a true sortal, but it can usually function as though it were.

There are plenty of other examples. Chop up an apple, a banana and a kiwi fruit and mix them together. Do you have one portion of fruit or three? Fill a pint glass with wine: is that one glass of wine or three, or four? Is Pink Floyd's *Dark Side of the Moon* one piece of music or ten? To think that there must be one and only one correct answer to each of these questions is absurd. The best answer is the one that gives the information the questioner is looking for.

That's why 'the radical claim that the topic of personal identity is strictly speaking non-existent' is not quite as radical it sounds. The clue is in the phrase 'strictly speaking'. You cannot have a strict philosophy of the identity of anything which is not a strict sortal concept. This claim is only disturbing if you think 'strict' is the same as 'rigorous'. We don't have to lapse into obfuscatory fog just because we reject the possibility of logical rigidity. It goes back to the idea that we can be as precise as possible without being totally precise.

The idea that we are creatures without a definite identity over time is the third and least-noticed aspect of the Ego Trick. The unity of sense of self it creates is so compelling that it becomes natural to think of ourselves as beings with clear boundaries in time and space, whose existence over time is all-or-nothing. This is false. We are fluid, ever-changing, amorphous selves. For practical purposes it's usually easy enough to say that we remain the same as we age, but we only need to think of early childhood or dementia to realise that this is not always the case. And when we then turn to look at more ordinary cases, we should be able to see that even over the course of a decade, without any major trauma, it is not true that we are strictly identical with our past selves.

This is what solves the riddle of the self I described in the introduction, that of continuity through change. We can remain the 'same' through great change because it is of the nature of persons that they change, and so our continued existence as the same person requires only that there is a steady enough process of change, not that we remain identical in any particular respect. It is because we are not pearls that we transform over time and can still be thought of as the same person over time.

The bundle view also makes sense of the cultural differences in conceptions of self we looked at in the previous chapter. Indeed, for the bundle theorist, such variation should not be surprising at all: if the self is not solid and fixed, it is only to be expected that there will be variations in which elements of the bundle come to the fore in different times and places. Different cultural variants of the self can all still be recognised as selves because the universal nature of the self is to be a changing yet connected flux.

These are the three central facts about ourselves that we have to accept, if we believe that the Ego Trick has done its job and created unified individuals out of a bundle of mental, neural and physical activity. First, the unity of the self is psychological. Second, we are no more than, but more than just, matter. And third, our identity is not what matters. Familiarity with this view has removed pretty much all the strangeness it might have had for me in the past. Oddly, however, the main question that remains is one posed by both critics and some supporters: if this is what the self is, then isn't the self an illusion?

'*You don't have to be afraid of your destruction because there is nothing to destroy.*'

Ringu Tulku, Tibetan Lama

8

Just an illusion?

Many years ago, I watched a documentary on spontaneous human combustion. As is typical for television treatments of so-called mysteries, it started by playing up the apparently inexplicable nature of the phenomenon, before going on to explain what really happens. Wilder cases were quickly debunked. Urban legends of drivers turning to see a passenger in a car next to them just burst into flames turned out to have no factual basis. The only genuine puzzles were cases where bodies were discovered burned to a char, but with little or no fire damage to anything around them. The most likely explanation of this turned out to be that a person's clothes may catch fire and the noxious fumes created could render them unconscious. Gruesome though it may sound, the fire may then begin to burn the person's body fat. Rather than rage out of control, however, as oxygen is burned up in the room, the fire may calm down to a steadier, low-flame burn, rather like a log in a wood burner when the airflow is reduced. For obvious reasons, this is known as the wick theory. This also explains why the legs of apparent victims of spontaneous human combustion are often found uncooked: they tend to have a low fat content.

A few days later, the programme came up in conversation with a man I knew, who had also watched it. 'Amazing thing, that spontaneous human combustion,' he remarked. 'People just bursting into flames for no apparent reason.'

My inattentive acquaintance had failed to spot the difference between *explaining something* and *explaining it away*. The TV programme had done the latter: it had shown that what appears to be spontaneous human combustion is no such thing.

There are those among both supporters and critics of bundle theories of the self who believe that such accounts do not so much explain what we are, as explain us away. Just as the wick theory explains the appearance of spontaneous human combustion but denies its reality, so bundle theories explain why it is we believe ourselves to be individual persons who exist over time, but deny that any such beings really exist. This radical idea has a history that goes back to the first bundle theory of all: that of the Buddha.

Anattā

Like any other old and geographically dispersed belief system, Buddhism ceased to be a singular system of thought many centuries ago. It is therefore impossible to say what *the* Buddhist conception of the self is. Nevertheless, the central concept of *anattā* – traditionally translated as 'no-self' – is important to all schools, and my interest in it is not that of a cataloguer of religious dogmas, but as a seeker for ideas that might shed light on who we are. What I'm interested in is its most credible reading, not its most authentic or popular one.

To help me find this, I spoke to Stephen Batchelor, who first trained in Geluk – one of the four Tibetan schools of Buddhism – which was founded by Tsongkhapa (1357-1419), widely considered to be the greatest of the Buddhist philosophers. Tsongkhapa's philosophy follows what is known as Madhyamaka – the middle way – between the nihilism of believing that nothing real exists and the view that ultimate reality is eternal and unchanging. Batchelor also went on to train in Zen in Korea. He is now best known as the author of *Buddhism Without Belief*, something of a cult classic, in which he attempted to strip Buddhist philosophy and practice of its supernatural, religious elements. More recently, he has stopped calling himself an agnostic, preferring the description contained in the title of his memoir, *Confessions of a Buddhist Atheist*.

Batchelor maintains that no-self, the hitherto standard translation of *anattā,* is almost certainly wrong. Many translators now prefer not-self, which may seem almost identical, but the small difference is significant. '*Attā* means "self", or *ātman* in Sanskrit, and then the *a-* is a privative,' Batchelor explained to me. 'To understand what not-self is, one first has to understand what is being denied,' to correctly identify what Tsongkhapa called 'the object of negation'.

So what is being negated in the word *attā*? To understand that, argues Batchelor, you have to appreciate the context of the Buddha's time, fourth-century BCE India, where *attā* or *ātman* was very much the central idea of the brahmanic tradition. That tradition thought of *brahman* as the impersonal idea of the deity, the ultimate reality, the transcendent, the unconditioned, absolute truth of things. There is a spark of that God within oneself. The true core of self is understood in terms of *ātman*, a unitary, partless, fundamental awareness or consciousness that is ultimately indistinguishable from the reality of *brahman*. Neither *ātman* nor *brahman*, however, has anything to do with the self as a distinct personality or ego.

So in brahmanic thought, as Batchelor puts it, 'the way in which a person through yogic practice liberates him- or herself from the travails of the suffering world and the round of reincarnation and so forth is by recognising that their true nature is not who they think they are – as a body, as a mind, as a series of thoughts, memories, perceptions, whatever it is – but rather that is an illusion or fiction in which you've somehow been tricked. You need therefore to return to a recognition of your true nature, your *ātman*, and in doing so you thereby achieve union with *brahman*. So when you die, you die in a state of absorption in which you are identified with your *ātman/brahman*. Then there is no more rebirth and when you die you are therefore reabsorbed into the divine itself, into union with god.'

Ātman is a kind of depersonalised self, lacking individual personality and identity. So if *ātman* succeeds in becoming fully reintegrated with *brahman*, personhood is destroyed. As the eastern philosophy scholar Chakravarthi Ram-Prasad explains, 'This is somewhat paradoxical: the self of the human person is truly and really what that person is, but that is precisely because the true self is more than – and lasts beyond – that person!'[1]

According to Stephen Batchelor, 'What the Buddha did was to reject that whole model altogether and declare that such an *ātman* effectively was a fiction, an illusion. So when he says *anattā*, he is rejecting the idea that there is an *ātman*, that there is a *brahman*, and focusing attention therefore on the phenomenal world. The Buddha's teaching is really about how we come to terms with the world of appearances. For him there is nothing behind the veil of appearances, there is simply an open field of impermanent and contingent and very often tragic suffering and painful events.'

The self that is denied in *anattā* is therefore only one very particular conception of self. That is quite different from denying any idea of self at all, which Batchelor claims the Buddha clearly does not do. 'In fact he uses the word *attā* in his discourses in a completely common-sense way. He talks of the *attā* as simply what we consider ourselves to be.' Batchelor points to a very famous passage in the *Dhammapada* (verse 80), in which the Buddha says: 'Well-makers lead the water (wherever they like); fletchers bend the arrow; carpenters bend a log of wood; wise people fashion themselves.'[2]

'In that usage,' says Batchelor, '*attā*, which is the same word, is not seen as problematic at all. In fact what the Buddha is pointing to is the notion of self as something like a project to be realised rather than something that inheres within you in some sort of transcendent way. So like a field to be cultivated, like an arrow to be fashioned, like a block of wood to be sculpted, so the person through their actions creates themselves. The Buddha's idea of self therefore is something that we create.

'Another fairly well-known passage says that a person is not born a Brahmin, a person is not born a farmer, but a person becomes a Brahmin, becomes a farmer, or becomes anything because of their karma, because of their actions. So you have what is nowadays sometimes called a performative conception of self. Your identity, your sense of being a person is formed through your actions, and that is only possible because there is not a fixed self. There is no unchanging essence or substance to which those attributes are then attached at all.'

Tsongkhapa scholar Thupten Jinpa agrees that 'the existence of the self as an independent, eternal and atemporal unifying principle is an illusion', but that the 'Madhyamaka dialectic does not negate the reality of our everyday world' and that 'Tsongkhapa is not rejecting in any way the validity of our commonsense notions of self and identity.'[3] Whether Batchelor's reading recovers the original intent of the Buddha is an interesting question, but for my purposes, truth and coherence matter more than doctrinal authenticity. When we look for that in Buddhism, we find that the most coherent readings of its teachings on not-self are indeed remarkably congruent with more recent bundle theories. The self is not an illusion. What is illusory is an idea of self which sees it as an unchanging, immortal essence. Strip that away and you are left, in Buddhism, with the 'five aggregates': body, feelings, perception, mental formations and consciousness. The self, as Batchelor puts it, 'is neither reducible to them nor can it be understood as existing independently of them.' No more than, but not just.

The moral of the story – 'that when you deny self you have to be very clear as to what is being rejected'– has a significance beyond Buddhism. If you look at any coherent claim to deny the self and ask exactly what is being denied, you will find it will not be denying the self completely. Only what is false and illusory should be denied, no more and no less. Realising that is a kind of enlightenment, even if it is not the way to nirvana.

Why then do many serious thinkers on the subject of the self persist with the vocabulary of illusion? When I put this question to the neuroscientist and practitioner of Zen Susan Blackmore, she replied: 'I was tempted to say, go and look in the dictionary. The dictionary definitions – and I've looked in lots of dictionaries for this purpose – are all pretty similar. An illusion is basically something that is not what it seems to be, or is in some way misleading, intellectually or perceptually. So when I say the self is an illusion, that's what I'm saying. And I think that is what the Buddha was saying – not that there's no such thing as a self, because in many contexts he would say there is, but that the self is not what it seems to be.'

The philosopher Daniel Dennett takes a similar line, calling the perception of a unitary controlling mind a 'veridical illusion'. 'It's an illusion in the same way the desktop on your computer is an illusion,' he told me. 'There aren't any little yellow files on your hard disc and in fact files are distributed, scattered all over your hard disk. All of the icons stand in for real and quite messy and elaborate processes – you really don't want to know anything about them. It's called the user illusion and that's a good term for it. I won't go so far as to say we're the only species with any kind of user illusion, but that's pretty close to the truth, I think.'

There is something important in what Dennett and Blackmore say. But we must avoid what Paul Ricoeur called 'the great oscillation that causes the "I" of the "I think" to appear, by turns, to be elevated inordinately to the heights of first truth and then cast down to the depths of a vast illusion'.[4] The self is an illusion, but not *just* an illusion. But still, I would prefer to do away with talk of illusion altogether. Talk of illusion suggests there is a way of perceiving oneself free from that illusion. But there isn't. Consider, for instance, the 'illusion' of a stick looking bent in a bucket of water. This was, for years, the paradigmatic example of a perceptual illusion used in philosophy. But as J.L. Austin pointed out, given the way the world is, a stick must appear bent in water. A really good magician's trick would be to make it look straight. Hence, as Austin put it, 'Familiarity takes the edge off illusion.'[5] Similarly, if we are to see ourselves as we really are, we will always see a self there. Ego-less experience is not somehow more veridical than ego experience. All we need to do is realise, when we see it, that like a bent stick in water, how it appears can be deceptive.

There's a neat example of this given by Douglas Hofstadter, another writer who is keen to talk of illusions, describing the self as 'a mirage that perceived itself, and of course it didn't believe that it was perceiving a mirage'.[6] He recounts an anecdote in which he pushed down on a pile of envelopes to pick them up and found, to his surprise, 'there was a marble sitting (or floating?) right in the middle of that flimsy cardboard box!'[7] Of course, it wasn't a marble at all. As he explains, 'for each envelope, at the vertex of the "V" made by its flap, there is a triple layer of paper as well as a thin layer of glue. An unintended consequence of this innocent design decision is that when you squeeze down on a hundred such envelopes all precisely aligned with each other, you can't compress that little zone as much as the other zones.' And that is a metaphor for the self: the feeling of a solid core which is created by nothing of the kind.

But the analogy undermines itself, because, of course, given the way the envelopes are made, what Hofstadter experiences when he presses down, he *must* experience. The feeling (resistance to compression) is entirely veridical: only the *interpretation* of the feeling (there is a marble there) is mistaken. He only goes wrong when he misinterprets what it is he's feeling. The same applies to the self. The unity and continuity we perceive are really there. We only go wrong when we interpret that as a unity and continuity of a single, solid thing.

Dennett acknowledges that there is a danger that the rejection of 'the self as an immutable pearl of magic stuff' could lead people to go too far. 'There's a stability and it's actually like the stability of everything else in this world. It's like the stability of the ship of Theseus. There's no core of the ship of Theseus, but there are some parts that last longer than others and there's an overall structure and if you keep replacing parts, you can come back in forty years and still recognise it, even though most of the parts have been replaced. What you're recognising is not just the parts that are still the very parts that you experienced before but the overall organisation of those parts, and even if every part was replaced, you'd still have the ship of Theseus.'

The problem with talk of illusion, I think, is that most people contrast illusory with real, so to say the self is an illusion is to imply it is not real. But it is. There is an Ego Trick, but it is not that the self doesn't exist, only that it is not what we generally assume it to be.

Perhaps the simplest analogy is with a cloud. From a distance it looks like an object with fairly clear edges, but the closer you get to it, the more indistinct it becomes. Get really close and you can see it's just a collection of water droplets. Does that mean clouds don't exist? Of course not. It just means that they are not chunks of cotton wool. The self is like a cloud that not only looks like a single object from the outside, but feels like one from the inside too. Knowing the truth doesn't change the way it either looks or feels, and nor does it con-jure it out of existence. It simply makes us recognise that at root each of us is an ever-changing flux, not a never-changing core. The solidity of self is an illusion; the self itself is not.

The Ego Trick is not to persuade us that we exist when we do not, but to make us believe we are more substantial and enduring than we really are. There may be an illusion as to *what* we really are, but not *that* we really are.

'There are people like me who just feel that they're effectively in the moment and they don't really think that the self that they are in the moment was there even a minute ago.'

Galen Strawson, philosopher

9

Reconstructing character

Pearl-like assumptions about the self are perhaps most stubborn when it comes to the idea of character. Almost everyone seems to believe that their personality is a consistent combination of traits which is, paradoxically, both unique and classifiable in any number of different schema. For instance, a great many people believe that their personality is a reflection of their astrological sign: that's why almost all online dating agencies and social networking sites include it in their profiles. Psychological profiling tests are always a big hit when printed in newspapers and magazines. The Myers–Briggs Type Indicator is widely used in recruitment, and people who take the test are usually convinced that the profile generated captures something about who they really are. Even Paul Ricoeur believes that in stability of character, 'the set of lasting dispositions by which a person is recognised', persons get closest to possessing the sameness (*idem*) over time that he argues we lack.[1]

Character has also made a comeback in moral philosophy in recent decades. Inspired largely by Aristotle, virtue theorists believe that inculcating certain habits and dispositions is central to being a good person. Ethics is not so much about following rules but becoming the kind of person who behaves well. Common sense reflects this thinking in various ways. When people are accused of horrible crimes, friends and relatives often rally with the complete conviction that 'he could never have done such a thing'. It is telling that when our preconceptions about how people will behave are confounded, we often respond by shrugging our shoulders and saying they acted 'out of character' more often than we question whether our character judgement was right in the first place.

The belief that character predicts action can be so strong that people sometimes confidently say they are certain how someone acted, even when they cannot possible know what they actually did. For instance, after Flight 93 crashed in Pennsylvania before it could reach its target in Washington on 9/11, some relatives of those who died were convinced that as 'men of action' they were sure to have acted to try to thwart the hijackers, even when there was no direct evidence that they did.[2]

What there is plenty of evidence for is that this confidence in our ability to know the characters of others, and ourselves, is misplaced. It would be absurd to deny that there is any predictability and stability to character. People who live together could hardly do so if they could not rely on each other to behave in consistently predictable ways, even though becoming a bit too predictable may drive them apart. Nevertheless, there is a lot of evidence that character is not quite as constant as we tend to assume. Importantly for this book, however, it is only as inconstant as bundle theories would suggest.

So how stable is character and how important is it in determining what we do? It is a truism to say that how we behave is a result of two factors: our own natures and the situations we find ourselves in. Many are now claiming, however, that it is situation, not character, which often makes the biggest difference to what we do. And if that is true, character is not as powerful a determinant of behaviour as most of us take it to be.

John Doris has assembled the most comprehensive case for this view in his book *Lack of Character*. Many of the experiments he cites have become widely known. In one, an actor drops a folder full of papers outside a phone booth, just as an unwitting experimental subject is stepping out. Some of these guinea pigs, however, have just had a pleasant but trivial surprise: the phone box was rigged so that an unexpected dime appeared in the coin-return slot at the end of the call. Of the 16 people who found the dime, 14 helped the actor pick up her papers. Of the 25 who didn't, only one did.[3] It would be an amazing fluke if the 14 who found the dime just happened to be more altruistic people. More likely is that, as other experiments have suggested, being put in a good mood, even by something small, makes people temporarily nicer. Character has nothing to do with it.

Another famous experiment saw subjects being asked to fill out a questionnaire in one building and then going to a second to give a short verbal presentation. Before changing site, however, some were told they were running late, some that they were just on time, and others that they were a little early. No suggestion was made that promptness was critical. On their way, the experimental subjects came across an actor slumped in a doorway, apparently in distress. How many stopped to help? 63 per cent of those who were early, 45 per cent of those on time, and only 10 per cent of people who were late.[4] Whether they helped did not depend primarily on whether they were generally kind, considerate people, but on whether they were in a hurry for something that didn't matter that much. What's more, these potential good Samaritans were all students at Princeton Theological Seminary.

More worryingly, our willingness to cause terrible harms also seems to be highly situation-dependent. Two classic studies stand out. In his notorious 'obedience experiments', Stanley Milgram asked subjects to deliver increasing levels of electric shock to someone in an adjoining room. In reality, the 'victim' was an actor and no shock was delivered, but the subjects didn't know this. The voltage delivered was increased by increments, with the dial labelled with ever more ominous markings such as 'extreme intensity shock' and 'danger: severe shock'. The actor next door would be screaming for the shocks to stop. Yet up to 93 per cent of the participants would follow the instructions to deliver the very highest level of shock.

The other infamous case is the Stanford Prison Experiment, in which Philip Zimbardo and his team simulated conditions in a prison with student volunteers taking on the roles of prisoners and guards. The two-week experiment was abandoned after six days, because the guards had descended into terrible cruelty, making prisoners clean out toilets with their bare hands and using fire extinguishers to hose down an insurrection. These were ordinary, decent people, turned sour by being placed in a position of power they could abuse.

What are we to conclude from these experiments and numerous others like them? I got the chance to ask Zimbardo about just this when I met him at a conference in Puebla, Mexico. Zimbardo had just demonstrated the dangers of stereotyping character when he started his talk on the psychology of evil and heroism by throwing away a cane he uses to help support his dodgy hip and dancing to Santana's *Change Your Evil Ways*, getting the audience to join him.

'There's the myth about human dignity and human character,' he told me over lunch. 'So we really want to believe that our actions all stem from some internal set of motives, of goodness, of morality, and courage, and they get perverted in certain situations for certain people. I start with a more simple model, to say that the human mind gives us templates or potentials to be anything at any time, and in fact, any time that somebody does something extraordinarily good or bad, it becomes imaginable for us.

'There was a wonderful cartoon in the *New Yorker*. It's two policemen, talking to each other, and one says to the other, "Like yourself, Jerome, I could be a good cop or a bad cop. I'm a complex amalgam of positive and negative personality traits that emerge or not depending on the circumstances." And that's really my whole approach.'

The power of situation to make people cross the moral line is perhaps best illustrated not by the students playing guards and prisoners in the experiment, but in what happened to the experimenter himself. Five days into the experiment, a former graduate student, Christina Maslach, who had just started dating Zimbardo, came down to see what was going on.

'More than fifty people had come down to the experiment at various points: psychologists from the department, graduate students, a public defender, a Catholic priest who'd been a prison chaplain,' says Zimbardo. 'Everybody said, "interesting simulation". She comes down five days into it, we are all now acclimated. This is what happens. I'm the prison superintendent, I have an itinerary. At ten o'clock at night, the guards line the prisoners up to take them to the toilet. This is the last time they can go to the toilet. After ten o'clock, if you have to go to the toilet you go in a bucket in the cell. But the guards developed a routine. They put bags over the prisoners' heads, they chain them together, they yell and curse and push them, and I look up and see this and for me, as the prison administrator, it's a check mark. It's the ten o'clock toilet run. There's no emotional impact. That's what happens. If it didn't happen I'd say, "What's happened? It's 10 o'clock."

'She sees this event and she begins to have tears, and I say, "Chris, look at this, isn't it interesting?" She doesn't say anything, so I say, "What's wrong with you? Don't you see, this is the crucible of human nature," whatever. I'm giving all the psychological jargon and she gets up and actually runs out. I run out after her and we're in front of the psychology department and she then says, "It's terrible what *you* are doing to those boys. They're not prisoners, they're not guards, they're boys, and you're responsible." So then I'm really arguing, I'm saying,

"What sort of psychologist are you?" I'm sure I said something like, "What kind of female reaction is this?" Then she said, "I'm not sure I want to continue our relationship, because I don't know who this is. You've changed. You're totally indifferent. How could you see these people suffering and not care? I always thought of you as a caring person but I don't know who you are." And I think it was that that made me realise I *had* changed.'

It had taken Zimbardo five days to fall into this mentality, and a furious hour-long argument to change his mind back. But, as is usually the case, having stepped back, he was in no sense corrupted for life. 'Most people, including all the research I know on Nazi guards, bounce back. The guards in the Stanford Prison study, who did horrendous things to other students, there was no carry over.'

It's worth stressing that although Zimbardo argues we have underestimated the power of social situations because we overestimate the power of individual dispositions, that does not mean he thinks people are not accountable for their behaviour. All the situational approach says is that we must take account of the mitigating circumstances.

For instance, Zimbardo spoke as an expert witness for the defence in the trial of Sergeant Chip Frederick, one of the American soldiers guilty of abuse in Iraq's Abu Ghraib prison. 'He did horrific things,' says Zimbardo, 'and I began my defence by saying, Sergeant Chip Frederick is guilty of the crimes he is charged with. However, what I want to present and document is that he never would have done those things, based on everything I know about him, except that he was in the situation that corrupted him. In fact, every single prison guard on the night shift did similar things, nine out of nine, and so you can't say this is a bad apple, that he is atypical. He was typical of everybody in that unique situation.

'The interesting thing is, no abuses at all happened on the day shift. Now why? Because on the day shift they had oversight, they had surveillance. On the night shift, in three months, no senior officer went down to the dungeon. They told these guards, do whatever you have to do to break the prisoners, prepare them for interrogation. So you had no restraint, no limit, and that's what you saw.'

Real-life cases like Abu Ghraib and experiments like those of Zimbardo led John Doris to conclude that 'situational factors are often better predictors of behaviour than personal factors . . . In very many situations it looks as though personality is less than robustly determinative of behaviour. To put things crudely, people typically lack character.'5

This conclusion goes against all common sense. But there is a well-known psychological phenomenon that helps explain why we might be too impressed by our apparent ability to describe people's characters in precise and reliable ways. The Forer Effect (often known as the Barnum Effect) is named after the psychologist who first demonstrated it in 1948. Forer simply showed a description of a personality to a number of subjects and asked them to rate how accurately it described them. On average, people rated it 4.26 out of 5 for accuracy. But each person had been given the same description, including phrases like 'You have a great need for other people to like and admire you,' 'You have a tendency to be critical of yourself,' and 'At times you are extroverted, affable, sociable, while at other times you are introverted, wary, reserved.'6 Character descriptions often seem persuasive because we notice what fits our self-image, overestimate the extent to which many descriptors are to some extent true of almost everyone, and disregard descriptions that don't fit. Given how easily we are taken in by the supposed accuracy of generic character traits, we should question the extent to which any list of character traits really captures us at all.

But surely, you might think, this does not mean we lack character completely. Isn't it absurd to say that there is no difference between, say, kind and mean people? It can't all hinge on whether you've found a coin that day. Character may not be as robust as we think it is, but it isn't that weak either, is it? The danger with this kind of response is that we are like relatives of thugs who see the evidence and simply stamp their feet and insist our Johnny could never have done such a thing. If we want to insist these experiments miss something, we have to explain what it is they've most certainly hit.

Saving character

The central truth is not that character is a myth, but that it varies more according to situation than we tend to assume. This means that, even if we take the findings at face value, a credible notion of character remains. Consider, for instance, a person's tendency to be generous or mean. The Doris critique says you can't just say that a person is mean or generous. The best you can do is to consider all the different kinds of situations a person would be in and ask if they would be mean or generous in each case. For the sake of simplicity, imagine you do this across a range of twelve typical situations. You might then generate the following character profile:

mean generous mean mean mean generous mean mean mean generous mean generous

There may be nothing inaccurate about calling this person mean, on the basis of his general tendency to be more mean than generous. Indeed, when we ordinarily apply character traits, we rarely believe that a person always acts according to it. A person can be affable but sometimes withdrawn, a brave fire-fighter may on some days be paralysed by fear, and a calm mother can occasionally lose her temper. The fact that there are some situations which can provoke behaviour contrary to what is normal does not mean we cannot talk of what is normal.

Now consider a person whose character profile, compiled on the same basis, contains seven counts of 'mean' and five of 'generous'.

This list, however, could be misleading, as it might be that the person is mean in seven unusual sets of circumstances but generous in five more common ones. So we need to weight the traits according to how frequently they are displayed, which we can do visually by means of altering letter size in a 'word cloud', where traits appear larger if they are displayed more frequently:

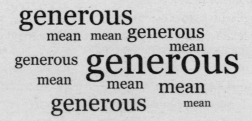

Such a person would be described as 'generous', not because they are always generous, but because there is a general trend towards generosity in most normal situations. This is still the case even though, in fact, there are more kinds of situation where they are mean than generous.

This might seem reasonable. It has, however, a discomforting corollary: the same person, with the same character, if now put into a life where a different range of situations was normal, could have the following cloud:

Now the overall description of the exact same person would be 'mean', not 'generous'. What this shows is that there is some contingency as to which descriptions of our characters are true. In other places at other times, a mean person could be generous, a brave one cowardly and so forth. This fits rather than contradicts common experience. Many German citizens, for instance, would have led blameless lives had they not lived under the Third Reich and been placed in situations which brought out their worse selves. Conversely, many people are able to live good, moral lives only because circumstances have not tested them.

You might think this saves the idea of character only at the price of completely transforming what it means. If character doesn't mean the tendency to display the same kind of traits across different situations, then it means nothing. Character without consistency is not character at all. There is clearly something to this, but one can still ask how much consistency character requires. As I've said, no one expects complete consistency.

What's more, the research Doris draws on does not establish that there is a complete absence of consistency in people's behaviours. The fact that character is a bad predictor of how someone will behave in any given novel situation does not mean that people don't generally display certain character traits across a range of situations. In fact, there is evidence that they do. Several attempts to analyse data on behaviour over a range of situations have suggested that there is significant stability of traits over different situations.[7] This alone is enough to show that the idea that character is just an illusion is far too simplistic.

But perhaps the most important limitations of character scepticism arise from a failure to distinguish between two senses of character, what I'll call *passive* and *active*. Passive character is the set of dispositions we just happen to have as a result of our genes, upbringing and experience, without any particular effort on our own part. Active character is the set of dispositions that we have because we've worked on developing them. To use a philosophical term of art, dispositions are active if they are the result of an individual's attempts at *self-constitution*, to build who they are.

You can't tell whether or not a disposition is passive or active in any given case just from knowing what it is. For instance, one person may be naturally reserved and another naturally outgoing. In both cases, this would be a reflection of their passive characters. But a third person may have decided that they should challenge their natural introversion and be more outgoing, and over time they may succeed. Their sociability would then be an active character trait, as I define it. Furthermore, a passive character trait can become an active one, if an individual chooses to strengthen and develop it. What may have initially been a kind of accident of birth and upbringing can be embraced and turned into something one nurtures in oneself. Finally, it should be clear that, in real life, traits are never purely active or passive. Rather, they tend to greater activeness the more they reflect deliberate efforts to mould our own behaviours.

With these two variables, what we normally talk of in the singular – character – can turn out to be quite different in different people. For some, character might be largely passive. For others, there may be a strong active component. For some, passive character traits might be highly variable across situations; for others, they might be very constant. The same is true of active character traits: people may be more or less successful in firmly entrenching desired traits.

For the sake of simplicity, we can crudely schematise any given individual's character into a hierarchy of types. The weakest kind of character traits are those which are passive and variable, neither self-chosen nor constant. Slightly more robust are passive, constant traits, which at least exhibit a kind of consistency. Next are active, variable traits, which, being self-chosen, are more fully 'ours' but lack constancy. The traits which are most 'characterful' are those which are both active and constant, ones we have in part chosen for ourselves and we display with a measure of consistency.

Every person will exhibit a mixture of these traits. Consider these four hypothetical examples:

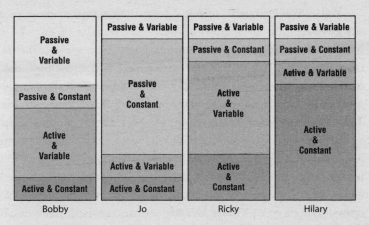

| Bobby | Jo | Ricky | Hilary |

Bobby might be thought to lack character in the sense that her traits are generally highly variable. Jo might be said to have character in the sense that her traits are generally constant, but to lack character in the sense that the personality is mostly not self-constituted. Ricky does have largely self-constituted character, but is still perhaps too inconsistent to be said to really have character. Only Hilary is a 'person of character' in the fullest sense: reasonably consistent over different situations with a character that is not just an accident of birth and upbringing.

If people are indeed variable in this way, then what would that predict for the kinds of studies that Doris cites? We would expect to find that only a minority of people are actually of consistent good character, and, likewise, only a few of consistent bad character. We would expect that character is often under-developed and that people would indeed behave differently according to circumstances. And that is precisely what the evidence does suggest. In almost all the examples given, it is not the case that the situation entirely determines the action. There is a small but significant percentage of people who always do the right (or wrong) thing, regardless of the changes in situation. Some of these do so purely because they happen to be so disposed, others because they have developed their characters in good or bad ways.

This is very important when we consider the idea of moral character. Those who emphasise the importance of situation are often critical of the virtue ethics tradition, which stresses the importance of developing moral character. Their critique is that if character is a myth, then virtue ethics rests on a myth. But the evidence they cite is based on the behaviour of a typical spread of people, only a minority of whom have the kind of moral character virtue ethics promotes, namely an ethical character disposed towards the good. Virtue ethics is not a theory about how most people actually make their moral choices, but a proposal for how we should set about making ourselves able to make better moral choices. Building moral character is a challenge, so the fact that the majority don't seem to have risen to it is not surprising.

Virtue may be rare. We might well find that most people are inconsistent in their virtuous behaviour, and their apparent generosity is easily switched off. This does not mean there is no value in trying to cultivate a generous personality: indeed, there may be even more. The evidence is that unless you try to cultivate traits, whether you display them will depend more on circumstances than on you. So consistency in character is something to be created; it does not arise organically.

Philip Zimbardo certainly thinks that we can and should learn from his research to build our own moral character. Indeed, he thinks there are some ways of building character that are remarkably simple. 'We know, if people label themselves in a certain way, that label comes to motivate behaviour. So if I tell you, "You know, of all the students I've ever had, when I look at your personality background, you're really very generous," the next week there's a blood drive, you're more likely to give blood.' His most recent project has been to get people, especially the young, to think of themselves as heroes in waiting, so that if they confront a situation where heroic action is required, they're ready to act accordingly.

Our knowledge of situationism should be used to build character more wisely, not to give up on it. For example, John Doris takes as one lesson the idea that we should avoid tempting situations rather than rely on character to enable us to resist temptation. The father of virtue ethics, Aristotle, agreed. He advised against getting drunk, for instance, for precisely the reason that we cannot rely on our inherent goodness to stop us from behaving badly if we're intoxicated. Likewise, a faithful spouse should avoid getting into situations that might tempt them into infidelity. To become the kind of person who avoids drunkenness or temptations of infidelity is precisely to develop virtuous character traits. Being of good character requires self-monitoring and sensitivity to context, not just relying on automatic behaviours. We can strive to be certain types of person but we should not expect to automatically behave according to whatever regulative ideal we set for ourselves.

Self-creation

If character has to be built in important ways, could one go further and say that identity itself is not just given, but is something we in some way create ourselves, by our actions? One of the most persistent recent advocates of this view is the philosopher Christine Korsgaard. Korsgaard criticises Parfit, and others like him, for seeing personal identity as being simply a matter of psychological connections and continuities. What she says is missing from this is an idea of which kinds of connections and continuities matter most for identity. The answer, says Korsgaard, is those which are the products of our actions and choices: 'Beliefs and desires you have actively arrived at are more truly your own than those which have simply arisen in you.'[8]

Agency – the individual's capacity to act – can perhaps explain some of the unity of self over time that a standard bundle view makes problematic. Take a long-term commitment like marriage. On a simple bundle view, wedding vows make no sense: I cannot bind my future self if that self is in a real sense not the same self as I am. But to be a person does not just mean to be whatever series of psychological connections and continuities endure; it is to commit oneself to making certain connections and continuities happen. In that sense, we can perhaps see the wedding vows as being even deeper than usually thought: it is not just that I promise to have and to hold, I promise to try to build future selves that will be able to maintain this vow. We do not so much promise *to be* good spouses as promise *to make ourselves into* good spouses.

Korsgaard's view puts the ethical where some see only the metaphysical. If what we are is not just given, we therefore have to choose what we become, and such choices have an ethical dimension, for we can choose to become faithful or faithless, honest or deceitful, generous or mean. 'We are responsible for our actions not because they are our products but because they are us, because we are what we do.'[9] However, her view is not an excessively romantic one. Self-creation is not heroic but necessary. 'Every human being must make himself into someone in particular, in order to have reasons to act and live. Carving out a personal identity for which we are responsible is one of the inescapable tasks of human life.'[10] Indeed, in order to do this, we have to adopt 'practical identities' which will define us socially, and these may be radically contingent. You can choose to become a mother, for instance, and there is nothing that meant you had to adopt that identity. Having made that choice, however, you have constructed an aspect of your identity which has ethical implications: '"I can't do that, it would be wrong" and "I can't do that, I'm his mother" are claims with the same structure.'[11]

Many other thinkers have also asserted the importance of agency in what Korsgaard calls self-constitution. Carol Rovane has argued that the set of psychological relations that comprise a person 'must include certain substantive practical commitments that serve as unifying projects',[12] a view Marya Schechtman accepts and builds on.[13] More portentously, Husserl wrote: 'The ego constitutes himself for himself in, so to speak, the unity of a history,' and 'Since, *by his own active generating*, the Ego constitutes himself as *identical substrate* of Ego properties, he constitutes himself also as a "fixed and abiding" personal Ego.'[14]

It is possible to make too much of agency. It is a common mistake to overestimate the importance of ideas that are new, or have been unjustly neglected. But agency is certainly something that is often missing from bundle accounts of the self. Just as there is no point in the brain where the self comes together, so there does not appear to be any one thing that unifies the self. Memory plays an important role, as can the creation of an autobiographical narrative. But action and agency do critical work too. For example, the project of writing this book arguably is more important for the unity of my self than the set of beliefs and ideas it contains and which I endorse. When I sat down to write it, my own beliefs were not held on file, permanently ready for inspection. I often don't remember my view about something: it is as though I have to think about the subject again in order to find out what I believe. But that doesn't bother me. No matter how jumbled my brain is in some ways, unity of agency only requires a reasonably stable set of intentions, and the ability to carry them through. By a combination of retrieval, reconstruction, adaptation and thinking anew, I am creating this book, and that has helped sustain and create the person I am.

However, this all does beg the question as to how unified a self *should* be. This is why the philosopher Galen Strawson strongly resists any view that says: not only *can* we create unity in the self in a certain way, we *ought* to do so, because unified selves are more fully selves than those that are less integrated. 'I think it's important that we should be allowed to be conflicted or inconsistent,' Strawson told me when I talked to him in the somewhat conflicted and inconsistent living room of his Oxford home. He describes the stance of 'people like Harry Frankfurt and Christine Korsgaard who think we have to be coherent and consistent' as 'a terrible kind of fascist view'. He swiftly recants. 'Not fascist, but it's as if they're trying to control something, regiment it. We should be allowed to be weak-willed and inconsistent. We should be catholic and eclectic.'

Strawson's counter points to what is perhaps the most important consequence of the bundle view. If the self is not a concrete, singular, stable thing, then we should not expect there to be only one way of being a self. If that's right, then virtually every theory of self and personal identity has inevitably gone wrong, because they have sought a description of selves which neatly fits all cases. But bundles can be tied together differently, more tightly and more loosely. This does not mean there are no general truths about selves at all. The nature of our bundles means there are constraints on what kinds of persons there can be. These constraints are sufficiently tight that we never come across other persons who are entirely alien to us. Nevertheless, within these constraints there may be far greater variations than we might have imagined.

Strawson is perhaps best known for his articulation of one such axis of variability in persons, between short- and long-termers, or what he calls episodics and diachronics. 'Here what I think you find is that people fall along a spectrum,' he told me. 'At one end of the spectrum there are the long-termers, who I call the diachronics, and they just naturally think that they're the same selves throughout their lives, and they really identify with themselves when they were children, say. And then there are these people who whenever they look back more than about five years, feel that it's not really them. And then moving to the other extreme, there are people who, like me, or how it seems to me, people who just feel that they're effectively in the moment and they don't really think that the self that they are in the moment was there even a minute ago.'

It seems that the main difficulty Strawson has in trying to persuade people of his view is that most are diachronic, and they just don't believe him when he claims to be an episodic. He's got plenty of examples that suggest he is far from alone. He quotes Emily Dickinson ('The mind is such a new place, last night feels obsolete'), Samuel Hanagid ('I have nothing in the world but the hour in which I am: it pauses for a moment, and then, like a cloud, moves on'), John Updike ('I have a persistent sensation, in my life and art, that I am just beginning') and countless others.

When people just don't believe him, it's often because they jump to conclusions about what life as an episodic must be like. For instance, what about long-term projects? No problem, says Strawson. 'It's just a fact that with everything I've written, I had a sentence, then I had two, then I stuck one in between the two, then I stuck another between. Things have always grown in that way. When I try to work, I usually open up my file, I really have no idea what I'm going to say, so I just read the last few paragraphs and then the next sentence comes. I don't know whether that's connected with being a short-termer but it's a real "how do I know what I think until I see what I say" experience.'

Nor are commitments problematic. 'Let me speak in the way that somebody might speak mockingly. The person who I will be tomorrow, or the next day, or in two weeks when I agreed to do something, will wake up feeling their obligation because they know someone else is depending on something. So there's just no problem at all. Those things are just inherited, completely smoothly.'

Strawson is not claiming that episodics have no sense of past or future at all, or no consistency. 'I do know that I, the human being, am very consistent in character,' he says, acknowledging both the persistence of the whole human being, Galen Strawson, and a certain kind of personality. He has a sense of his self, but he doesn't identify

171

this with this persisting human animal. He's relatively indifferent to its past and future, and this is temperamental, it's not philosophical. 'I found these things in my diaries saying things like "I have no narrative sense of self at all", so I've got some nice evidence that this was [what] it was like to me before I might have been corrupted by philosophical thinking about it.'

Could it be that the same individual can be episodic in some situations, diachronic in others? Strawson thinks so, and cites embarrassment as a good example. 'If I think of something really embarrassing I did even five years ago, somehow I relive it – that metaphor is a really good metaphor – you literally relive it as if you're just as embarrassed now as you were then, whereas if you're thinking of something else it may seem really remote from you. The other example I have, going the other way, is that when I think of my death I seem to think that it's me who's going to die, me as I am now, whereas when I think of my future life, which is obviously not as far away as my death, I don't have a sense that there's going to be a me there at all. You could say that shows I'm inconsistent, but I think the way you put it is better, that it depends partly on what you're thinking about.'

It seems to me that Strawson's theory is ripe for empirical testing. We should go out and see whether or not people do line up on an episodic–diachronic spectrum, as he believes. It seems very likely to me that they do. But in some ways, for present purposes, that doesn't matter. The main point is that there is surely some variation in how selves experience themselves, and there is not just one way of being a person. This finding is not exactly predicted by the bundle view, but it is entirely congruent with it. Accepting the bundle theory should prime you to accept that other people may experience their selves very differently to how you do. There are more ways of being a person than meets the I.

PART THREE

Our Future Selves

It might sound disappointing to go diving for pearls and come up with tangled, messy bundles. But if that is what lies beneath our surfaces, we have to get on and make the most of what we have found. And not all that is precious impresses at first sight: more people have got rich mining coal than diamonds, and oil moves more machinery than gold.

So how do we move forward with the knowledge that our true nature is less substantial and more fluid than most people have believed? What does it mean for the prospect of life after death? What does it mean for life *before* death? And what implications are there for the future of society?

'Who I am is unintelligible apart from the notion that I will cease, that what I am is something that is moving inexorably towards its end.'

Stephen Batchelor, atheist Buddhist

10

Life after death

The banks of the River Esk in south-west Scotland provide an unlikely spot for the first Tibetan Buddhist centre in the West. Founded in 1967 by Chögyam Trungpa Rinpoche and Akong Tulku Rinpoche, Kagyu Samye Ling is physical proof of Tibetan Buddhism's appeal to westerners and its curious ability to adapt itself to local tastes in some ways, while remaining thoroughly alien in others.

In its gift shop, for example, you can buy a tasteful mug – one of which sits full of tea beside me right now – as well as a set of feng shui Buddhas, a pairing as nonsensical as a putting Ganesha in a nativity scene. You can also contemplate spiritual truths while sipping cappuccino and munching on a *pain au chocolat* in the cafe, while electrically powered prayer wheels ensure a constant supply of good karma.

Despite Samye Ling's apparently easy accommodation to modern life, any attentive visitor cannot help noticing that Buddhism is not just a philosophy, but a religion as superstitious as any other. The impressive stupa, for example, is a temple-like structure described as utilising 'a 2,500-year-old spiritual technology' which 'creates an energy field that purifies and balances the internal and external five elements that compose the universe'. It is claimed that the one at Samye Ling contains a grain of the Buddha's bone and other relics from highly realised lamas and tulkus. Those who are not so holy need not worry, however: 'for a minimum donation of £500 you can have your ashes placed in the Stupa'. Since 'this ceremonial is the appropriate procedure for ensuring a good rebirth', that's surely a very good investment.

The stupa, feng shui Buddhas and prayer wheels deeply disappointed me. I don't suffer from the seemingly common delusion that Tibetans are spiritually superior to the rest of humankind, but I have found Buddhist philosophy to be a rich intellectual tradition. Yet its often profoundly rational thought sits alongside other ideas which seem to be no more than outdated superstitions. Conceptions of self are a case in point. Like many, I have been struck by the similarities between western bundle theories of the self and Buddhism's doctrine of *anattā*, which we looked at in Chapter Eight. Nevertheless, Buddhists also believe in reincarnation. But how can a rational view of the self as a kind of temporary construction be compatible with the supernatural view of the self as something that can transfer from one body to another?

That's why I was at Samye Ling: to talk to Akong Tulku Rinpoche, a lama who is supposed to be a reincarnation of a specific historical person. If the idea of reincarnation made any sense, then I had to look at its most credible version; a tradition which also advocated *anattā* clearly was not unsophisticated in its understanding of what we are. I wanted to find out what it really meant for someone who sincerely believed he was a reincarnation. Not just any of the numerous King Arthurs to be found wandering around Glastonbury, but someone whose belief is rooted in a respectable intellectual tradition.

Akong received me in a room that had the size and feel of a prefabricated primary-school classroom. A piece of electronic equipment kept bleeping steadily throughout our conversation, occasionally accompanied by a fax machine whirring into life. Halfway up one of the room's long sides, Akong had carved out a little sacred space. He sat cross-legged on his 'bed' – a lightly decorated wooden bench, with a small carved table in front of him. With a tartan blanket covering his legs, checked shirt and quilted jacket, he lacked the aura of other-worldliness that so often seems to be enough by itself to convince people of a religious leader's holiness.

As we talked, Akong ran through prayer beads and repeatedly turned over the pages of a *pe-cha*, a Tibetan loose-leafed book which probably contained the text of a ritual, perhaps for blessing the statue that sat on the table in front of him. Students often bring such statues to their lama for consecration. It would be tempting to assume that he was either not paying much attention to me or, more likely, just going through the motions with the rituals. After all, if prayer wheels can be turned by electric motors, it surely can't matter much whether such practices are undertaken with full care and attention. But it is possible that Akong was demonstrating one of the claimed benefits of what he called Buddhist 'mind-training': a greater sensitivity to all aspects of your experience. 'If you are driving a car you don't have accidents,' he told me. 'You can see your road, you can see the landscape, you can have conversations with others all at the same time.' Far from removing us from the hubbub of modern life, it seems mindfulness training can actually make us more effective multitaskers.

Akong is believed to be the latest reincarnation of a specific spiritual leader, or lama. In Akong's case, his lineage only goes back one generation: he is said to be the first reincarnation of the first Akong. As he explained to me, 'In Buddhism, everybody is a reincarnation. But there are different levels of reincarnation. Some choose what kind of home they want to be reincarnated in, in order to help others. Some are reincarnated without their own wishes because of their past karmic accumulations.'

In the case of tulkus – 'highly realised' lamas who are able to choose their own reincarnation – some leave letters or other instructions to tell their followers where to find their reincarnation. Others don't, and it is for the disciples to go to a 'high person who has the capability to know where to look for the child'. Such a person is 'spiritually developed enough to be capable of recollecting the parent's past and future without any kind of shadow'.

'So the monastery then went to look for that particular child,' he explains. 'Maybe two or three children are very similar, then you take the list back to the same person and the same person says which is the right child you are looking for. I am that kind.'

Revealingly, however, there is an absence of any semblance of a personal relationship between Akong II and Akong I. Most obviously, Akong says of his previous life, 'I don't remember anything.' For him, all that matters is that everybody says he is the first reincarnation of Akong, and that means he must have the same qualities. 'Then I have to serve the best that I can for the benefit of people whenever I can. I'm not here to investigate the first Akong.'

Nor does he give any thought to who his successor will be: 'That is up to the others.' All he is interested in doing is 'to try to develop loving kindness and compassion as much as possible, and try to meditate as much as you can'. That way, death will not be suffering but like 'trying to change house'.

Another tulku, Ringu Tulku Rinpoche, is even more circumspect about his reincarnation story. I had met Ringu in the home of a personal development coach who combined neuro-linguistic programming, Tibetan Buddhist meditation and sometimes 'equine-assisted learning'. It is not at all unusual to find people picking and mixing from the Buddhist tradition in this way, and most Buddhists seem to be perfectly happy for people to help themselves to whatever in their spiritual toolkit seems to work for them. Ringu had just arrived after a long drive from London, and was sitting in the conservatory in a sleeveless saffron shirt. Ringu says that the whole idea of reincarnation is 'just Tibetan culture'. As he explains, the idea of lines of reincarnated lamas is not something that goes back more than two millennia to the life of the Buddha, but one that actually only started in the twelfth century with the Karmapa lama (nearly two centuries, incidentally, before the first Dalai Lama). 'The first Karmapa, when he died, said, "I have to come back, because my teacher asked me to build this monastery." So after some time a boy came and said "I am Karmapa."'

Ringu goes on to give me an account of the first three Karmapas which seems on checking to be a little jumbled up. But the precise details don't matter because it is clear that history and myth are very much intertwined anyway. Stories tell of child prodigies, mothers hearing chants coming from the tulku still in the womb, miracles performed in the court of Kublai Khan and so on. The significant point is that once the Karmapa lama started being reincarnated, everyone else wanted to get in on the act.

'It became like a system that if your teacher is supposed to be a highly realised being then his students would try to find his reincarnation, and Tibet became full of tulkus,' said Ringu. 'So some of them may be true reincarnations, some of them maybe not so much, so we don't know exactly.'

The system doesn't sound very reliable, I tell Ringu. While the old tales talk of miracles and memories, that's not normal now, if it ever was. For instance, does he remember things from a past life?

'No. That's why I'm thinking in my case it's a mistake,' he says, and laughs.

Does he know of any people who have genuine reliable memory of past lives?

'Some people say they do. I don't know, I can't say whether that's exactly true or not. The present Karmapa says something interesting, that when he sees a photo or something like that of the last Karmapa, he remembers what happened then, but not like he was the Karmapa, but like he was kind of there.'

The present Karmapa is an interesting example to cite, because there's a dispute within the Kagyu school of Tibetan Budhism as to who he actually is. Most accept that the seventeenth Karmapa is Ogyen Trinley Dorje, but others – including the fourteenth Sharmapa, who has traditionally been mainly responsible for identifying the Karmapa – believe it is Trinley Thaye Dorje. The result is that we now have two competing Karmapas.

Akong and Ringu's lack of any felt connection with their previous incarnations, the absence of any clear evidence that someone even is a reincarnation, and the no-self doctrine of *anattā*: all these suggest that, whatever reincarnation is supposed to be, it is not about the survival of the self in any standard sense. Yet not only do Buddhists believe that something continues from one life to the next, but that thing is the continuation of a named individual. How can this make sense?

Akong's explanation starts with the assertion that on the Buddhist view of ultimate reality, there is no distinction between self and other. 'Each individual is part of everybody,' he tells me. 'We are all the same mind, part of the same thing. We are not divided.'

How is it then that individuals are reincarnated? There must be some sense in which there is a distinction between self and other, otherwise there could be no rebirth, nor any karmic consequences for individuals of their actions.

One answer strikes me as little more than a clever linguistic trick. Ringu argued from the premise of *anattā* that there is no thing which is the self. 'If there was one thing truly that was existing then you could destroy it, then it's finished,' he says, 'but because it is not like that, there is nothing you can destroy.' In other words, because you cannot destroy something which is no-thing, no-things are indestructible. That means that since the self is a no-thing, it too cannot be destroyed by death and so can reasonably be thought to survive it.

This is no better than the riddle I was told as a child: if having a sandwich is better than nothing, but nothing is better than being master of the universe, then having a jam sandwich is better than being master of the universe. Whether we're talking about selves or sandwiches, the trick is to take nothing – the absence of a thing – and treat it as though it were a kind of thing after all – an indestructible no-thing.

Akong offers a better explanation of what might survive death by use of an analogy. Ultimate reality is like an empty space. Individuals are like buildings occupying a part of this space. The end of a life is like the demolishing of a building, but then we build another – our next life – around the same emptiness. And if you do that, you have the same land and same atmosphere, which is why the karma follows you. The habits you follow in one life follow you to the next.

The analogy neatly draws out a fundamental distinction between the Buddhist view of the self and the dominant one in the western tradition. For in a sense, I think of myself as the building, not the space. The building is what gives shape and coherence to a particular life: personality, memory, body and the largely conscious connections of experience. This is similar to Janet's dementia metaphor in Chapter Three, in which I am the layers of the onion, not just the solid pearl at the centre. But for Akong, these aren't the most important things at all. What really matters are the habits that are practised inside the building, and which give the space a strange kind of character that persists even once the walls have come tumbling down.

Ringu puts the same idea in a slightly different way. That which continues from one life to the next is not the contents of consciousness, such as memories or knowledge of people and places, but the mind's 'habitual tendencies'. So if, for example, you have practised mindfulness enough to have extreme mental clarity, then that clarity will be there in your reincarnation. 'If anything continues, I think what would continue are my habitual tendencies, the way I react, the way I think. That is what would probably continue, not necessarily all the memories, because lots of things we forget even now.'

What we seem to have here is a threefold distinction between the ultimate unified reality; the relative reality of individuals in each mortal lifespan (*skandhas* or 'aggregates'); and the intermediate reality of the 'mindstream', persisting mainly as habits, which are the subjects of karmic laws. To put it another way, if we accept the Tibetan Buddhist view, we have three kinds of selves: the building, the space occupied by a series of buildings, and the entire space of which the building only occupies a part.

But, on this analogy, I would argue that only the building has the coherence required for anything to which we can meaningfully apply the pronoun 'I'. Of course, you could say that is the point: reincarnation is not of the 'I'. But this concession is swiftly undermined by the fact that the doctrine of reincarnation requires that whatever comes back as the karmic locus – that which reaps the consequences of past actions – must in some meaningful sense be the *same person*. The problem is that the 'space' Akong describes does not seem to be in any substantive way the same person over time. To put it another way, Buddhism needs to deny the personal nature of reincarnation in order to make it coherent, but assert its personal nature in order to make it ethical.

In practice, Buddhists seem to be ambivalent about the extent to which reincarnation is personal. For instance, many insist that even the terms 'rebirth' and 'reincarnation' are misleading, and that 'mindstream emanation' is better. Against those who insist on this, I should point out that both Ringu and Akong used only the 'incorrect' terminology. But the very idea of 'mindstream' is that of the moment-to-moment continuity (*samtāna*) of awareness. So whether you call it an emanation or a reincarnation, each subsequent life does seem to be continuing a flow of awareness that is, in the ordinary run of things, personal and individual. 'Mindstream emanation' may sound impersonal, but what it refers to certainly is not.

Akong certainly seems to be ambivalent about how much he sees his emanations as really being him. As we have seen, he does not appear to have any personal interest in his past or future incarnations. Rather than being a rebirth of self, it is as if you inherit the habits and karma of your predecessor and you try to leave a decent legacy to the next person in the chain. But, in other ways, Akong does talk as though it will really be *him* in the next life. 'Death is trying to change another house. If I want a good house then I have to accumulate good karma, positive things.'

Ringu also slips between impersonal and personal views of his various incarnations. His most explicit statements simply concern the continuation of habitual tendencies. But other comments imply a sense of self that does not seem coherent without memory. For instance, when I ask him about what death means to him, he says: 'I don't know exactly how it is, we don't remember things.' But then he says he thinks it might be like sleep. 'You wake up in a different body, with a different awareness. In a way our body is a little like that. The body that we have before we sleep and the one we wake up with is not exactly the same. So I don't see there is much problem that it could be similar, [though] not exactly [the same].' Although he adds later that habitual tendencies rather than memories are probably the things 'I find will be more prominent if I wake,' it is of course not possible to have the sense of waking up in a new body unless you have a strong sense of having fallen asleep in an old one. It seems that one cannot think about reincarnation without at some stage making an assumption that it is in some important sense just like the continuation of the self from day to day in this life, when clearly it couldn't be like that.

This is where I think the doctrine of reincarnation gets slippery. On the one hand, for it to make any sense, it clearly can't involve the straightforward transference of one life to another body. You have a set of memories, plans, projects, friends and family. All of these things do not continue in whatever the next life is. So there is *something* which is obliterated at death and does not continue, something which seems to be very important to who we are. People like Akong seem to accept this, which is why they talk about spaces and buildings. Yet it is not difficult to elicit certain trains of thought – such as the karmic consequences on future incarnations of our present actions – which seem to make these spaces much more building-like after all.

Most tellingly, perhaps, despite the disavowal of the importance of memory across lives, Buddhists seem very attached to the idea that it is both possible and actual. It is as though Buddhism needs to offer at least the hope of even a trace of 'ordinary survival' to be appealing. So, when I pointed out to Akong that clearly most people have no memories of past lives, he replied: 'Many people do. There are many books with experiences of previous life. Some people may not have, many people have. Maybe once every year you may have particular memories. There is nobody who has never had memories.' He also uses past-life memory as an explanation for why some people are particularly gifted. 'You learn something and you inherit something . . . Some six- or seven-year-old children can write books or poetry.'

Ringu also has his amazing tales of past-life recall, such as that of a young girl in Scotland who would always scream and shout if she was put into a car. Then, when she could speak, she announced she was not called her birth name, and that she remembered a car accident in which her friend was killed.

Here we move from conceptual coherence to empirical evidence, and despite the numerous books and testimonies Akong and Ringu cite, as the old saying goes, the plural of anecdote is not data. If someone had really remembered a detail from a past life which could be verified and they could not have otherwise known, that would be an astonishing discovery, on a par with making contact with extraterrestrial life. And if people did routinely recall past lives, it shouldn't be hard to find numerous verifiable instances of such memories. But what we actually find are only unproven, astonishing claims or 'memories' which do not require genuine memory at all, merely the acquisition of key information.

To give just one example: in Martin Scorsese's film *Kundun*, we are presented with the dramatisation of the search for the reincarnation of the Dalai Lama. Possible candidates are identified by a crack team of lamas, and are then tested by their ability to identify objects owned by the previous Dalai Lama. One succeeds and is thereby deemed to be the true incarnation.

It is only a film, of course, and I think it is unlikely that the real events were so clear-cut. But let's just imagine they were. What would that prove? The first thing to consider is that the child does not have anything like access to a repository of memories. The test is to identify objects belonging to the previous Dalai Lama. If the boy simply remembered the past life, the lama squad could have just asked him to tell them things about life in the monastery.

So what we have is not a test of memory, but a one-off test of object selection. It could be argued that if you test enough children, eventually one will choose correctly just by chance. But a better explanation is based on the fact that the lamas who know the right answers are in the room at the time of the test. Without necessarily adopting a deliberate strategy, a child could sense from the reactions of the group which object should be his settled choice. This is not remotely fanciful: even horses can do as much. In the early twentieth century, one called Clever Hans appeared to be able to do some basic arithmetic, repeatedly and reliably tapping his hoof the same number of times as the right answer to a sum set for him to solve. When investigated, it was discovered that Hans was actually responding to changes in the posture and expression of onlookers, who visibly relaxed when he got to the right number. What psychologists call the Clever Hans Effect might well be what enables a child to correctly identify the lama's possessions.

At this point, true believers will respond: 'But what about the case of X?' or just: 'There are too many such reports for them to all be false.' But you could say the same about ghosts, UFOs, saintly visitations, alien abductions or the efficacy of innumerable quack medicines. There is no global anti-Buddhist conspiracy. If there were good evidence, plenty of people would be interested in verifying it and dealing with its consequences.

There is another problem with the doctrine of reincarnation which is not so much empirical as moral. I think it strange that so many people seem to find the ideas of karma and rebirth comforting, for there is certainly a dark side to the whole notion. Akong says, 'Of course some karmic habits are inherited habits.' On his view, even our genetic inheritance is the result of karmic action. 'You may say, "I have this sickness because my father is sick, and therefore it's nothing to do with the karma, it's to do with my parent's gene."' But you got the parents you have because of your actions in your past life. 'You yourself have a connection to that particular person because that's your karmic pattern. So therefore you can't say this is only parents, but this is very much due to your actions.' In other words, to say anything other than that people who have genetically inherited illnesses deserve them is an evasion of the harsh truth.

Of course, the truth may indeed be harsh, so this is not in itself evidence against the claims of reincarnation. But such evidence is not needed, because the case against is already solid. In the first place, there is simply no good reason to believe that any habitual tendencies or other karmic loci do transfer from one life to the next. It is often considered disrespectful to dismiss any aspects of religion as mere superstitions, but if that is what they are, there is no other truthful way of putting it.

But even if for whatever reason you think there is, or may be, something to this idea, such a form of reincarnation cannot provide for the survival of the individual from one life to the next. Even if there is another mind emanation of Akong, the individual, particular person Akong Rinpoche will die. It is clutching at straws to suggest that the mere continuation of habitual tendencies is enough to ensure survival of the person. After all, a person can acquire many such tendencies from their parents, but our parents only live on in us in a loose, metaphorical sense. Reincarnation in the context of *anattā*, even if it takes place, is certainly nothing like survival of the self in any ordinary sense – and that is not in itself a criticism of Buddhism, but simply a description of its claims.

Buddhism is not the only major religion which holds some kind of belief in life after death, however. The idea is central to most faiths, and is certainly at the heart of the one I was loosely brought up in, Christianity. Could we not find here a credible conception of the self which offers the promise of an existence after our mortal frame has done its work? As with Buddhism, the answer turns out to be more complicated than the question.

Resurrection

Having dismissed the idea that we have immaterial souls, you might assume that there is nothing left to be said for the Christian idea of a life to come. However, I was surprised to discover that many Christians, including Pope Benedict XVI, do not believe in the dualist soul of Descartes or Richard Swinburne. Far from being a core creed of Christianity, it is arguably not authentically Christian at all. Rather, as the Christian psychologist Warren S. Brown puts it, many Christians see the person 'as a unitary physical entity without a separate nonphysical soul, but not reducible to "nothing but" the physiology of cells of the chemistry of molecules'.[1] This is very much like the kind of material person I described in Chapter Seven: we are no more than, but more than just, matter.

In the Hebrew Bible it is certainly the case that the relatively few references to resurrection are clearly bodily. 'Thy dead men shall live, together with my dead body shall they arise. Awake and sing, ye that dwell in dust,' it is written in Isaiah 26:19. 'Thus saith the Lord God,' in Ezekial 37:12, 'Behold, O my people, I will open your graves, and cause you to come up out of your graves.' Theologians and religious historians generally agree that the New Testament and the Early Church fathers did not talk about souls leaving fresh corpses either, but only of a resurrection of the body. In the Christian tradition, human beings are essentially embodied beings. Jesus's own return from the dead in bodily form provided the template for the vision of a life to come for all, at least those who were saved. Aquinas, for instance, believed in the existence of immaterial souls but wrote, 'Soul is not the whole human being, only part of one: my Soul is not me.'[2] Little wonder that the future Pope Benedict, then Cardinal Ratzinger, could write nearly 800 years later: 'We have discovered anew the indivisibility of man. We live our corporeality with a new intensity and experience it as the indispensable way of realizing the one being of man.'[3]

I met with Justin Thacker, head of theology at the Evangelical Alliance, who explains that the word 'soul' in the New Testament is usually a translation of the Greek word *psuchê*, which it is generally agreed does not necessarily apply to what Thacker describes as 'a kind of detachable non-material part of me'. Aristotle, for instance, talks about *psuchê* and many scholars believe that he did not think it referred to an immaterial object, but a kind of organisation of matter which makes it function as a living thing. It's somewhat similar to the way we now think about life. Many used to think that life was a kind of separate force that had to be 'breathed into' inanimate matter. Now we accept that life occurs simply when matter becomes sufficiently ordered and self-replicating. Soul is somewhat like this and, since each person functions uniquely, for Thacker, soul is 'the essential me, the thing that makes me *me*. My soul, my *psuchê*, is just my life, my personality, who I am.'

Catholics and Protestants sing from the same hymn sheet on this. 'Scripture contains no word denoting only the body (separated and distinguished from the soul),' wrote Ratzinger, 'while conversely in the vast majority of cases the word soul, too, means the whole corporeally existing man.'[4]

One corollary of this view is that, as Thacker puts it, 'it is not remotely the case that the soul has its own inherent immortality. Basically God makes the call after death whether we survive or not. Immortality is a gift of God, and it's a gift of God after death, it's not a gift of God at birth.' Ratzinger again is in accord. 'The Greek doctrine of the immortality of the soul . . . is wrongly regarded as a Christian idea, too.'[5] As a Polish Catholic theologian described it to me, Christians look forward to everlasting life, life without beginning or end, as that is the preserve of the deity.

It is true that many Christians have thought and do think that the soul is indeed a separate, immortal non-physical entity. But this view, argues Thacker, is a corruption of the original Christian idea, for which we can blame the influences of Greek philosophy – especially Pythagoras and Plato – and, more recently, Descartes. Both Plato and Descartes talked of an essential, immaterial, detachable core of self, although interestingly Raymond Martin and John Barresi claim that Descartes was the first major thinker to call this mind (*mens*) rather than soul (*anima*).[6]

But if the Platonic–Cartesian soul is not authentically Christian, how did it get so mixed up in that religion? The truth is that Greek influences were there very early on in Christianity's history and so have been deeply entangled since the earliest Church thought. As Warren S. Brown says, much of the New Testament was expressed 'within first-century habits of thought, which were strongly influenced by a Hellenized view of human nature'.[7]

If we reject dualism and believe that bodily resurrection is necessary for an afterlife, do we have any good reasons to think it will happen? The idea is clearly a hard sell in the contemporary world. You might well ask, 'Is this not all completely absurd, quite contrary to our understanding of matter and its modes of behaviour, and therefore hopelessly mythological?' If you're Joseph Ratzinger, you have indeed asked just that, in exactly those words.[8]

It would seem to be good news for Christians if their religion didn't commit them to a dualistic view of the mind, but fully embraced the necessity of embodiment. If you are going to believe in the life of the self after death, it's a good idea to start with a conception of the self that is in step with our best knowledge about what people are. But as the old song goes, it's not how you start, it's how you finish, and Christians like Thacker take this idea far from the sound ground of science and experience and into the realms of speculative faith.

First of all, although we are given new resurrection bodies, which are physical, when it comes to 'how God is going to do that and what's going to happen,' says Thacker, 'I don't know.' That's not necessarily a fatal admission. After all, why should we know all God's ways and means? But at the very least it does gloss over an important question. God could not resurrect us using the very same atoms that comprised us on Earth, partly because these change over our lifetimes anyway, and partly because the same atoms would have ended up in several people over the millennia of human existence.

This problem was recognised in Christianity's earliest days, with ingenious but wild solutions proposed for it. The second-century Christian apologist Athenagoras, for instance, considered the argument that the food chain made it inevitable that humans would end up in part constituted by bits of other humans. As he put it, 'When animals of the kind suitable for human food, which have fed on the bodies of men, pass through their stomach, and become incorporated with the bodies of those who have partaken of them, it is an absolute necessity, they say, that the parts of the bodies of men which have served as nourishment to the animals which have partaken of them should pass into other bodies of men.' His solution was that 'it is very plain that none of the things contrary to nature can be united with those bodies for which it is not a suitable and correspondent nourishment, but either passes off by the bowels before it produces some other humour, crude and corrupted; or, if it continue for a longer time, produces suffering or disease hard to cure, destroying at the same time the natural nourishment, or even the flesh itself which needs nourishment.'[9] In other words, any bits of other humans that you ate would inevitably find their way out into the sewers.

A more common, and more plausible, strategy has been to accept that there will be some mixing of the basic matter out of which we are made, and to accept the consequence that God would have to use new atoms when resurrecting us. As Brown puts it, 'our eternal existence would not be the continuation of some aspect of our current embodiment but would be a new creation, outside of the time and space we currently occupy'.[10] This invites the question: would the resulting person be a resurrection or a replica?

Then there is the question of what exactly this self is, which is to be resurrected, and what happens to it between death and the final judgement. 'It's incredibly hard to know what is going on during that period of time, ontologically,' admits Thacker. This appears to be a hot theological issue, of the kind which makes atheists giggle with glee at the seemingly medieval absurdity of it. Ratzinger clearly rejects the Lutheran view of the 'sleep of death', in which the dead lack any consciousness at all until the final resurrection. But as to what exactly this intermediate state is like, most theologians appear to be justifiably baffled. 'The closest I can say is that in some sense God keeps us,' says Thacker. 'Somehow – I don't know how – God maintains his relationship with me across time.' Thacker and Ratzinger both believe that, as the former puts it, 'fundamentally who we are as people, as persons, is relational. Who I am is who I am in relation to God.' Is this mysterious, confusing or just confused?

Perhaps the most serious difficulty is that for all the apparent familiarity of corporeal life after death, these bodies turn out to be unlike any physical bodies we know. As St Paul put it, 'It is sown a natural body; it is raised a spiritual body. There is a natural body, and there is a spiritual body.'[11] The Early Church fathers developed this view that bodies that are resurrected are transformed by the process into something more fitting for eternal life. Origen, for instance, wrote in the second century that 'God's command restores out of the earthly and animal body a spiritual one, capable of inhabiting the heavens.'[12]

This view persists today among those who believe in a bodily res-urrection. Of our resurrection, Ratzinger writes, 'it would require immortal bodies needing no sustenance and a completely different condition of matter'.[13] For Thacker, Jesus is 'the paradigm, the model for our resurrection bodies' and as such it is clear that 'the form of physicality that Jesus had is also a different kind of physicality. In many ways it was normal – he ate fish, he invited Thomas to touch him, he said "see that I am flesh and blood, I'm not a ghost, I'm not a spirit." But at the same time he did just appear through walls. At first he was unrecognisable, for instance, by the two on the road to Emmaus. Tom Wright, the Bishop of Durham, calls it a trans-physicality, which means it's physical, but it's a different kind of physicality to the physicality we have.'

This seems to me something of a have-cake-and-eat-it scenario. The theologians accept what secular science strongly suggests – that we are physical beings – but then talk about a kind of physicality that is unlike any other, one which allows for walking through walls.

It sounds reasonable to be told that the bodies are just like the bodies we have, apart from X, Y and Z. But if X, Y and Z turn out to be central features of matter, the glib 'apart from' takes on a greater significance. It's like being told that you're going on holiday to somewhere that is just like the Bahamas, apart from the fact it's cold, wet and there are no beaches.

For instance, the nature of all flesh is that it is perishable and corruptible. Thacker is right to say that it is conceivable that we could have pretty much the same bodies, only ones that didn't age. As we'll see, there are serious scientists trying to work out how to switch off ageing in real humans. But other vulnerabilities seem to be more essentially tied to our physical nature. Most obviously, bodies can be injured. If I accidentally cut off my own head while chopping wood in paradise, what happens then? It sounds like a flippant question, but if there is no good answer, the coherence of the idea of a transphysical body disappears. Thacker has a stab at an answer, but I don't find it convincing. What looks to me like a huge chasm at the heart of his conception of the self is only leaped over with the aid of faith.

'In relation to injuries and so on, I can only imagine that in the new heavens and new earth, which is how I understand eternal life, however God works it, God will ensure that injuries do not accrue and that the body we have is one that doesn't age, is incorruptible, and won't have any bacterial viruses – except the healthy kind presumably – that cause us disease and so on. How God does that? This is absolutely at the limits of what I know. All I know is that the Bible presents this image, this picture, to us of the perfect heaven and new earth where there's no more pain and suffering, disease and death.'

For anyone who lacks the sure faith to simply trust that things must turn out as they are described in the Bible, no matter how incoherent they may seem to us, the traditional Christian idea of the physical resurrection of the dead seems implausible, if not entirely impossible. The dilemma is simple: the price you pay for accepting the essentially embodied nature of human beings is that such bodies are not and could not be reconstructed perhaps centuries after death and made immortal. The price you pay for saying that they are like our present bodies, only radically different in certain key respects, is that you place a huge mystery where an explanation should be. If I wanted eternal life, I would not be happy to bet on an eschatological resurrection.

Of course, as Thacker freely admits, there is no universal agreement about what souls are among Christians, even evangelicals. Thacker thinks his view is the predominant one among evangelicals in the academy, and it is striking how much Protestant evangelicals agree with Roman Catholics on this issue. In the pews, Thacker thinks most people assume a kind of Cartesian dualism, but their faith doesn't hang on that. In the pulpits, he's more circumspect. 'In my forty years of being an evangelical, probably thirty years of remembering sermons, I don't think I've heard a single sermon on the soul.' Preachers tend to steer clear because it is all rather murky and complicated. This may seem reasonable, but in some ways I think it's quite damning. Christianity's great promise is of a life after death, reconciled with our maker. So if it can't give a clear account of what that life will be like, it's guilty of avoiding a defence of its most important central claim. Lack of clarity about self and soul is therefore not an inevitable result of the subject's complexity, it's a symptom of a gaping hole at the centre of the Christian message.

For committed Christians like Thacker, however, this debate is not settled by secular philosophising, but in the faith and experience he has of Christ, whose resurrection is all the proof that is needed.

'If there is a conflict between contemporary science and God, then God wins every time,' says Thacker, adding that 'God has revealed himself to us through the Bible.' He accepts that the Bible has to be interpreted, but 'there are some things which I think the Bible is unbelievably clear about and that have scientific consequences. Let's take the resurrection of Jesus Christ. If science somehow – and I can't even imagine how – but if it told me that the resurrection of Jesus Christ was just categorically impossible, could not happen, I would disbelieve that and continue to believe what the Bible teaches about the resurrection of Jesus Christ, because if you take away the resurrection there is no Christian faith, it just doesn't exist.'

It's worth stressing this point because this is not just Thacker's view. Many, if not most, people of faith start from that faith even when thinking about issues which can be approached in an entirely secular way. And if you want to understand why people believe what they do, you first have to identify what beliefs act as their bedrocks. For many Christians, that bedrock is the Bible, a personal experience of God or Christ, or some combination of the two. And if that is the case, that means they do not approach issues such as the nature of soul and self as objective enquirers after truth. When they reason about the issue, reason is in the service of faith and does not simply follow the argument wherever it may lead.

For those of us without such faith, the conclusion seems clear and beyond reasonable doubt. We have no reason to suppose that reincarnation takes place and, even if it did, we have no reason to believe that it would result in the continued life of individual persons. Nor do we have any reason to believe that we can look forward to a resurrection of the body which will give us life after death. On any credible view of the self, its existence ends with the death of the body. And we can't do anything about that – or at least, not yet . . .

*'People romanticise death and ageing in order to put it out of their minds
and get on with their miserably short lives.'*

Aubrey de Grey, biomedical gerontologist

11

The future of the self

It is often said that the primary purpose of fiction set in the future is not to speculate about what possibly will be, but to shine a light on our human nature in the present. If that is so, it is telling that so many writers have imagined worlds in which 'human nature' is no longer one thing. We see people divided into genetically modified 'valids' and inferior, purely natural 'in-valids' (*Gatacca*); we see five different castes of human – Alphas, Betas, Gammas, Deltas and Epsilons – selectively bred for mindless or intelligent tasks (*Brave New World*); we see working and middle classes evolve over millennia into two different species, Eloi and Morlocks (*The Time Machine*); and we see human beings whose entire experience is a virtual reality, while their real bodies are kept alive in pods by intelligent machines who harvest their bioelectrical energy (*The Matrix*).

These dystopias are readily imaginable only because at some level it is obvious that human nature need not be set in stone, and that there is no reason in principle why creatures like ourselves might not become radically different. Until recently, such mutations were simply abstract possibilities, within the power only of Gods, sorcerers and novelists. Over recent decades, however, we have begun to consider more seriously the possibility that technology might change us more in a generation or two than evolution has done over millions of years. We may have finally understood what the self is, just in time to see it completely reconstructed.

The potential changes we could face range from the relatively minor to the mind-bogglingly radical. At the less dramatic end of the spectrum, for instance, Rita Carter, whom we met in Chapter Five, believes that 'everything that is happening in society today is shifting us towards multiplicity'. Children grow up without the uniformity and consistency of experience which used to form them into conventional, strongly singular personalities. 'Everything's exploded in the last twenty years. You will get people who, even if they still live in the same community and a very stable family situation, are subject to a thousand different cultures every time they walk out of the door. Every one of those impacts produces a slither of new personality because you have to respond to the world and that's how personalities get made.' Carter does not see this as a bad thing. 'Those very integrated people, I think, are becoming dinosaurs. I don't think they're very well equipped to deal with a multicultural, very fast moving, very dynamic sort of culture they might have to move in now.'

I've already explained why I think the multiplicity thesis can easily be overstated, but Carter is surely right to say that the way in which the world is changing is conducive to more multi-facetedness and less rigid, fixed notions of who we are. But that is, I think, a relatively minor shift in the balance of characteristics of selves we are already familiar with, not a major transformation. Could other changes go even deeper?

Sleepwalking to oblivion

'The more sensationalist media has "brain scientist says we're all doomed" or "doing computers rots your brain, is bad for your brain".' So complained the neuroscientist and then head of the Royal

Institution, Baroness Susan Greenfield, when I interviewed her on stage at the Bristol Festival of Ideas in 2009. Headlines show she was not exaggerating:

SOCIAL WEBSITES HARM CHILDREN'S BRAINS:
CHILLING WARNING TO PARENTS FROM TOP NEUROSCIENTIST

FACEBOOK AND BEBO RISK 'INFANTILISING' THE HUMAN MIND

SOCIETY HARD–WIRED FOR A FALL[1]

'I'm not saying that at all,' she protested, 'but I am saying that will be true if we just let things take their own course and we don't think about what's happening and what we want.' That's not so much a denial as an insistence on the important difference between a categorical claim and a warning of the possible.

Greenfield has received a lot of flak from colleagues for her self-confessed speculative musings on how the very nature of human identity might change. Nevertheless, although many of her specific worries may be exaggerated or misplaced, she is a senior brain scientist, and her understanding of what might make radical transformation possible is worth listening to.

'Although most neuroscientists are familiar with the concept of what we call plasticity,' she told me, 'it might be that most people haven't really grasped just how malleable their own brains are, how sensitive their brains are to the environment.' Given that, she is fascinated by 'how the unquestionably different environment of computer games and sustained exposure to a screen might change the brain in ways that have not happened before, because we've never had this kind of experience over sustained periods of time before.'

This has a direct relation to what the self actually is. Keen to stress that what she offers is 'a perspective which is complementary to, but doesn't contradict, those of philosophers, anthropologists, sociologists and the like', she understand the self as essentially 'the personalisation of the brain' through the unique connections each cerebrum makes.

'When you're born, you're born with pretty much all the brain cells you'll ever have, but it's the growth of the connections between those brain cells that accounts for the growth of the brain after birth. So, even if you're a clone – that means an identical twin – you will have a unique configuration of brain-cell connections because they are driven by your unique experiences.'

This should be uncontroversial stuff with which almost all neuroscientists would agree. Where Greenfield gets a little more speculative is when she imagines the variations in types of selves which might emerge if different kinds of connections become dominant. She bases this speculation on what I think is a quite useful way of simplifying three forms of subjective experience.

The first she calls the 'Someone' scenario, which is the normal case of 'you being different from someone else'. This is how we almost all, almost always, feel ourselves to be. 'In brain terms, the Someone scenario could be reflected in the forging of idiosyncratic connections, and associations that are unique to your particular experiences, and also leave you open to modification by those.'

Although we tend to think of ourselves as Someones, we are on occasion also 'Anyones', the second of her scenarios. 'Sometimes in our everyday life, we're all parts of a team, it's where we subsume our own interests, our own individuality, we sacrifice what we personally want to do in favour of the group.' Instead of 'living out an individual life story', Anyone lives out a collective life story. Although this is benign in moderation, Anyones are malign when they are created by ideologies in which 'you are so constrained in what you do, what you think, what you eat, how you live out your life, what your agenda is, that really you're subsuming your life into the collective life story of that particular ideology . . . You're living out life as a component, you're just a small part in the very big picture, to the extent that in extreme scenarios, as we know tragically happens at the moment, the individual can be disposed of or can dispose of themselves in the service of the greater narrative.' The neural basis of this could be that there are 'connections that are so strong that they are more resistant to modification by subsequent experience'.

We also sometimes live life under the third scenario, as Nobodies. 'Human beings have stalked this planet for 100,000 years, [and] we have from time to time indulged in wine, women and song; or, drugs and sex and rock and roll, the modern equivalent. There are moments in most of our lives when we want to "let ourselves go", "blow our minds". The very word "ecstasy" in Greek means to stand outside of yourself. These are moments when we abrogate our sense of self, when we are no longer self-conscious, we're just conscious.' This is what psychologists call depersonalisation.

Dancing is one of Greenfield's favourite examples. 'The whole point of dancing is that you *let yourself go*. You're having a *sensational* time, that is to say you're putting a premium once again on the senses, as you would as a small child, you're back in the booming, buzzing confusion.' What's interesting about the feeling of being Nobody is that it can be wonderful and dreadful. For instance, most people who take marijuana report depersonalisation effects, sometimes quite strongly, and find them pleasant. But as Roy J. Matthew points out, in clinical psychology 'depersonalisation is associated with such unpleasant states of mind as fatigue, sleep deprivation, sensory deprivation, anxiety, depression, temporal lobe migraine, temporal lobe epilepsy and so on'.[2] Depersonalisation disorder is a recognised, distressing condition.

Greenfield's worry is that the future is Nobody's. 'It's an interesting paradox of the human condition, that up until now, we've oscillated between these two scenarios, one in which we want to be fulfilled, we want to set ourselves goals, we want to be different from other people, we want to have a life narrative, we want life to have a meaning . . . but at the same time we've wanted sometimes to stand back from that and let ourselves go . . . Up until now, we've enjoyed doing this, a lot, but if someone said to you, "I want to do that all the time, I want to go to the rave every single moment I'm alive," on the whole, we'd feel rather sorry for someone like that, just as we'd feel sorry for someone that proudly declared they'd never let their hair down, they'd never let themselves go, they'd never had a sensational time in their lives.'

The route from here to this dystopia seems very unclear. Greenfield bases her worries on the idea that screen culture is essentially 'sensational', that it bombards us with discrete experiences which do not forge the kinds of connections that make us into Someones. She seems to think that sitting in front of a computer renders the user passive. But actually it is much more demanding than the television, its predecessor as the destroyer of western civilisation. Even 'shoot 'em up' games are highly complex these days. They do not fit Greenfield's caricature: 'you press a button and something explodes in your face, and you press another button and something else happens, and you press another button and something else happens, at a very fast pace'. Screen culture is more about chatting and twittering than it is boom-bang-a-bang.

Nevertheless, combine her reminder that our brains are indeed elastic; her plausible claim that we are all part Someone, part Anyone and part Nobody; and the fact that we are going to be able to alter our brains more in the future than we have done in the past, and then at the very least we do have a kind of model for thinking about which directions certain changes could take us. Greenfield notes that the Someone scenario is the dominant modern, western one, suggesting that in other times and places, a higher premium could be placed on being Anyone or Nobody. To assume that the future is Someone's is therefore to assume too much. If we value the kind of individuality being Someone allows, then we may have to fight social and technological forces that might undermine it.

Methuselitis

'Please raise your hand if you want to get Alzheimer's disease.' Aubrey de Grey often asks this at public talks, and on this occasion, as usual, no one took up the invitation. Nor are people much keener to develop any of the other diseases of old age. Wouldn't it be great, therefore, if we could cure them? To do that, however, we'd have to be able to switch off senescence – biological ageing – itself. That would have a not insignificant 'side-benefit': indefinite longevity. Only disease, accident or the end of the world itself would stop us from being immortal.

De Grey is all in favour. As chairman and chief science officer of his Methuselah Foundation, he is funding and bringing together research on what he calls Strategies for Engineered Negligible Senescence (SENS). For many, the longevity side-benefit is more arresting than the main show, but de Grey considers this fixation irrational and claims he's 'not particularly' interested in living a long time. As he told me when I met him at a philosophy festival in Hay-on-Wye, where he was politely received by a somewhat bemused, sceptical public, 'a large part of the reason why I don't want to die any time soon is because I'm healthy; furthermore, I want to stay healthy for as long as I live. So if I want to stay healthy for as long as I live, and I want to live as long as I stay healthy, then, you know . . .' The implications don't need spelling out.

Many people believe it's pointless thinking about this because it just ain't going to happen. We don't even have a cure for most cancers, let alone the capacity to arrest all the biological mechanisms that cause age-related sickness. De Grey finds this negativity defeatist. As long as it is a realistic possibility, it doesn't even have to be the most probable outcome for us to want to work towards it. Nor do we need to find all the solutions in order to start living much longer. De Grey has come up with a notion he calls 'longevity escape velocity'. If you're lucky enough to be alive when your further degeneration can be postponed for twenty years, then the chances are that before those two decades are up, further advances will have been made, and you'll get, say, another thirty years. In that time, more progress will be made, and so on. That's why de Grey has made the famous, or perhaps notorious, claim: 'The first person to live to 1,000 might be 60 already.'

De Grey is unquestionably a maverick, the most optimistic advocate for the claims of biogerontology. In 2005, twenty-eight biogerontologists went so far as to co-sign a rebuttal to a paper he published in the journal *EMBO Reports*. 'Each one of the specific proposals that comprises the SENS agenda is, at our present state of ignorance, extremely optimistic,' they wrote. 'A research programme based around the SENS agenda . . . is so far from plausible that it commands no respect at all from within the scientific community.'[3]

But de Grey is confident that the tide of opinion will change when we achieve 'robust mouse rejuvenation'. 'I reckon that conservatively what we're going to need to do is take mice that are already naturally pretty long-lived, which would typically mean that they live up to three years; do nothing whatsoever to them until they reach the age of two, so they're already middle-aged; and then add a couple of more years to their lifespan by doing sufficiently comprehensive rejuvenation to them that they keep going in a healthy state. That, I think, would definitely be decisive enough that nobody could really continue to deny that regenerative medicine can be practically applied to ageing.' De Grey is in no doubt that it will happen, and even goes so far as to say: 'We're definitely looking at between six and eight years with at least 50 per cent probability of getting to that point which I've just described.'

Whether he is right or not, we have already seen incremental increases to lifespan that are quite remarkable. In a paper for the major medical journal *The Lancet*, a team of Danish scientists wrote: 'If the pace of increase in life expectancy in developed countries over the past two centuries continues through the 21st century, most babies born since 2000 in France, Germany, Italy, the UK, the USA, Canada, Japan, and other countries with long life expectancies will celebrate their 100th birthdays.'[4] In the UK in 1901, in contrast, life expectancy at birth was 45 for boys and 49 for girls.[5]

So even if de Grey is wildly optimistic, significantly longer life does seem to be a real possibility in the not-so-distant future. Would this change what it means to be a person? 'I don't think it's going to transform what it is to be a person at all, no,' says de Grey, who is generally dismissive of any existential worries raised by much greater longevity. 'What it is to be a person is, I think, defined by how we live our lives when we don't have to worry about our health; in other words, how we live our lives when we are young adults.' So when people talk about facing up to mortality as something deeply built in to the human condition, perhaps quoting Heidegger on being-towards-death, that's just romantic nonsense? 'That's absolutely right. I couldn't have put it better myself.'

De Grey thinks that the problem we have is that we're caught in a 'pro-ageing trance'. 'People romanticise death and ageing in order to put it out of their minds and get on with their miserably short lives and make the best of them rather than be preoccupied by this terrible thing that's going to happen. It makes perfect sense while there is genuinely nothing that you're going to be able to do about it for even the remotely foreseeable future. But as soon as that ceases to be true, it becomes an enormous part of the problem.'

The pro-ageing trance means that we see as immutable facts of life things which are really just accidental consequences of our current short lives. So, for instance, we think of life's progression from youth, through middle age, to old age as being deeply embedded in what it means to live a good life. 'It's certainly deeply embedded in our notion of what life is at the moment,' says de Grey, 'but I think it's romantic nonsense, to quote you, to suggest that it's necessarily embedded; in other words that it is somehow superior to be that way than to live in a world in which age matters much less.'

De Grey is entertainingly scathing about any suggestion that it is important to be mindful of our mortality. 'I think it's a rather tedious topic, to be perfectly honest.' Asked whether making death rarer would make it easier for us to hide from our mortality, he just answers, 'And your point is?' To the suggestion that mortality is the single most important fact of life, he proposes that beer is, for him, a more credible candidate. And in response to the suggestion that a sense of life's finitude is partly what enables people to have a richer appreciation of life in the here and now, he says: 'Not in the slightest, no.'

The transhumanist Nick Bostrom, whom we'll meet shortly, makes similar points in slightly less pugilistic ways. Even if death is the most important fact of life, he insists it is 'not the meaning-giving one. That seems the height of rationalisation. There are people who don't think they will die. There are people who think they will be reincarnated, people who think they will have eternal life in an after-life, there are probably some people who thought that by having some elixir or something they could stop the ageing process. It doesn't seem that their lives are therefore necessarily meaningless. It just seems very implausible that these occasional thoughts people have about death are the sole thing on which the meaning of their lives depends.'

But isn't the very coherence of the idea of radically extended life put into question by the bundle theory? With no immutable essence of self, if I lived for 500 years the extent to which it would even make sense to talk about that person as being the same as me would be questionable.

'I think it's questionable already, at the level of fifty years, or even twenty years,' says de Grey. 'It doesn't bother me in the slightest. The main thing is, I'm not interested in getting sick, I'm not interested in other people getting sick.' The fact remains that at any given point, if we are healthy, we will want to go on living. It doesn't matter if that means that what goes on living changes over time to eventually become a different person. At any given moment, if a person has the opportunity to keep on living healthily, why wouldn't anyone take it?

One answer is boredom. The late Bernard Williams wrote a now famous paper based on *The Makropulos Case*, a play by Karel Čapek, later adapted into an opera by Janáček. The central character is known as E.M., having had several names over her lifetime with those initials. In the sixteenth century, her father, a court physician, tried out an elixir of life on her. Now aged 342, 'her unending life has come to a state of boredom, indifference and coldness'. She eventually refuses to keep taking the elixir and dies, miserable, showing that it is possible to die too late, as well as too soon. If he lived too long, Williams concludes his paper, 'I would eventually have had altogether too much of myself.'[6]

'It's pathetic, isn't it?' retorts de Grey, 'I mean, honestly. It's a matter of education, which is one reason why adult education is going to be so important. If you haven't been given the wherewithal to get the most out of life, then people don't know what to do with a life that's ten years long, they spend it sitting in front of the television. But if one has a proper education, one never runs out of things to do. I've got at least a 1,000-year backlog already of things I haven't done and by the time I'm through it I'll have at least another 1,000. There is a lot to do in the world.'

I don't expect to achieve longevity escape velocity, and I'm not sure that we will ever be able to live for as long as de Grey believes is possible. But much longer life does indeed seem a real possibility. Where I think de Grey is right is that although it would present all sorts of new challenges for how to live a good life, it wouldn't fundamentally change what it means to be a person.

If I had to make one prediction about a society of Methuselahs, however, it would be this: the bundle view would come to be seen as intuitively the right one. Over a life lasting hundreds of years, the

claim that there is no immutable essence of self, and that our identities gradually change over time, so that we eventually become quite
different people, will not need to be argued for: experience will show
it to be obviously true. The idiom 'that was a lifetime ago' will res-
onate more deeply, and will be superseded by 'that was several
lifetimes ago'. What it means to be a person will not change, it will
just become clearer.

Transhumanism

Many of the kinds of real-life personal transformation we've considered so far are quite radical. We've seen a man with multiple-
personality disorder, a woman who lost all sense of self because of a
brain tumour, a man who could not lay down any new memories for
fifty-five years, two men who became women, and ordinary, decent
students who became vicious despots in an experiment. In each case,
we've been wondering to what extent the individual person can survive such transformations. Well, pretty soon such agonising might
seem rather quaint. Compared to the changes to come, we might
look like people worrying about the odd pothole the day before our
city is bombed into oblivion. When it comes to transforming the self,
things could soon start getting much, much more radical.

That is the view of so-called transhumanists. Among the scenarios
many consider likely are not just a vast increase in lifespan, but the
replacement of part, or all, of the organic brain with synthetic replace-
ments, accelerating and/or increasing the brain's capacities by massive
orders of magnitude, and uploading your self to live in a virtual reality. It sounds completely potty, but transhumanism is not a movement
of cranks – or at least, it contains no more than you'd find in any other
collection of academics and enthusiasts. One of its leading lights is Nick
Bostrom, who heads the Future of Humanity Institute at Oxford
University, a transhumanist citadel at the heart of academe.

Bostrom thinks that the kinds of questions of personal identity I've been exploring in this book 'might become more practically important in the future than they are today, because there is only a limited extent to which you actually can change your mind and body today. You can have a religious conversion, perhaps, or maybe a sex-change operation, and these are exceptional cases. But the greater the actual capability you have to change yourself radically, the more important potentially these questions about personal identity could become.'

Take, for instance, 'superintelligence'. One version of this is called weak superintelligence, which is running ordinary human intelligence at much faster rates, either by speeding up the brain or by uploading it to a faster machine. The subjective effect of this, it is supposed, is to slow down the perceived passage of time. If your mind is working ten times faster, then time seems to pass ten times more slowly. It seems impossible to imagine what life would be like after such a change. Walking a mile would feel like walking ten, eating lunch might take what seems to be three hours. It could be even worse. 'If the speed-up was very great, say, an upload that runs a million times faster than a human being, then a lot of mesoscopic [between microscopic and macroscopic] human reality would be excruciatingly slow.' So what's the solution? 'You'd either want to live in a virtual reality, where things could keep pace with your mind, or you'd perhaps want to shrink yourself down to the molecular level, where things happen much faster in real reality.' A more attractive option, perhaps, what Bostrom calls the ideal scenario, is 'one where we had the opportunity to do this at our own pace. So, in principle, once you're an upload, you could run it at normal speed, you wouldn't have to speed it up right away; or you could have a virtual reality that was very similar to the current reality, to minimise this future shock. From there on, you could perhaps take small steps to modify that in ways you found desirable, so that you could continue to grow over years and decades, try out new capabilities, but you wouldn't feel you had to rush to do that to keep up with the cutting edge.'

Are you horrified, excited, or both? Neither? There's more. Uploading is perhaps the most extraordinary possibility. The central premise is that if your sense of self and identity is essentially the result of the unique set of connections in your brain, then in principle it might be possible to replicate these connections in something else, something that may be a kind of computer. It should be said that many question whether this could ever be practically or even theoretically possible. Science fiction has been playing with the idea for some time, but the idea that it could be a reality in our lifetimes takes some getting used to.

Bostrom, however, sees no reason why in principle uploading should present any problem. 'Speaking for myself, there is a clear sense in which there is a degree of independence between your personal survival and the underlying stuff. We know the atoms of your body are swapped out over a lifetime. You eat, those atoms in your food replace the atoms in your body. This occurs on an ongoing basis and we don't think of that as a problem. You wouldn't benefit if you could somehow wrap yourself up in plastic and prevent the atoms from being exchanged. I'm not sure that the uploading scenario is fundamentally any different from an accelerated metabolic process where the atoms in your body are substituted for other atoms.'

Indeed, in some versions, you would be uploaded to a computer that would be housed inside your organic body. As a thought experiment, Bostrom asks us to imagine that, in fact, a scientist did this last night while you were asleep. 'Suppose he kept your same body but inserted a little computer instead of your brain that was running an upload of you, but hooked up to all your sensory organs in such a way that, to you, the world appeared unchanged, and, in fact, your causal relations to the world were unchanged. Then it's not clear to me how that would matter at all.'

Imagine being uploaded to a virtual reality, however, and it gets harder to conceive how that would actually affect us. 'Obviously if you have an upload who then lives in a very different world, and it's just a virtual reality where everything is very different, it might feel disorientating,' says Bostrom, casually. 'There might be all sorts of new possibilities that would affect it psychologically in such a way that it would turn into a different type of person.'

What I find extraordinary about all this is that the people who are seriously considering it don't seem to be worried about the potential these changes have to effectively destroy who we currently are. They are almost misanthropic in their zeal: if it eliminates human beings as we know them, so much the better. We're a pretty rubbish species anyway. Bostrom expresses this thought in a somewhat more positive way when he says that 'the important thing is not to be human, but to be humane'.[7]

'It's a slogan, but it basically points out that not all things about being human are great. History and psychology amply illustrate the different bad things about being human. So then there is a tendency to define "human" in such a way that it only captures what is good about humans: perhaps a little bit of naughtiness, but no gas chambers. That seems like a useless enterprise. We may as well distinguish two words: one, describing what we are, descriptively, "human", some good parts and some bad parts; and another word – let's call it "humane", but you could choose another word for it – which describes what we ought to be or what we could become if things went ideally well for us. And the basic point is that these are not identical.'

He sees no problem with our turning into something different. If those successors are better, why not do it? 'People might have desires for all sorts of things other than their own preservation . . . It might be that people could care about descendents of themselves, that is, later version of themselves, that bore some similarity to their present self, or were linked in some way like a chain to their present self, without actually being their selves, and they might still have some personal reason to care about them that they wouldn't have to some other arbitrary entity.

'The way I think about it is that we have a model at hand, which is the transition from child to adult, which is very profound. We have vastly greater capacities as adults than as children and our whole mental lives are different, our preoccupations, yet we don't think it is bad for a child to grow up. So that seems to show it is possible to have at least that degree of radical transformation without it necessarily being bad for the person who undergoes it. So you could think of adults as being stymied stages in the development of a greater adult, at a posthuman level of development, that we can't currently reach.'

Whether we like this or not, we really should start thinking seriously about the changes technology could make to who and what we are. Superintelligence and uploading may be far off, but other ways of changing us are already happening. Drugs like Viagra and Cialis can be seen in this light as precursors for more radical drugs that could change the very pattern of our desires. Pharmaceutical companies are already working on the 'female Viagra', which is not designed to correct physiological malfunction but to boost libido. Biological interventions could even affect the extent to which we are monogamous or promiscuous, as experiments on genetically engineered voles suggest.

'There are two kinds of these voles in the wild,' Bostrom explains, 'meadow voles and mountain voles, and one of them is naturally monogamous and one is polygamous. So they took the one that was polygamous and by changing this one gene they could make it monogamous, and presumably vice-versa. It might be possible that the human system is more complicated than that of the vole, that more genes are responsible for regulating the degree to which we are promiscuous or monogamous, but there might be analogous things with either hormones or other interventions you could perhaps relatively easily switch.' Such innovations may come sooner rather than later. 'Something like this could potentially be achieved with a pill, within a decade or two.'

The people around at the dawn of these choices are going to have more control about how they pan out than people later down the line. A very conservative culture, for example, could create the kind of society, where people are monogamous and want to be, which would then be perpetuated indefinitely. In contrast, if changes had been effected in 1960s California perhaps we'd all now be in a society of free love. A certain generation in the future could have disproportionate power over the future of humanity. So although it may sound as if we would be taking control of our desires, in fact once we change our desires, the ones we then have would drive what we did next. Bostrom agrees.

'Yeah. I think that, partly for that reason, the modifications that affect our emotions, values and preferences are ones we should be particularly careful with, because if you get it wrong, according to our current lights even, you might not then want to change it back. You'd have the capability of changing it back, you'd have the technology, but you wouldn't have the desire. So there could definitely be this lock-in effect, where you set off down some track and then you would never want to go back. But there could be several different tracks we could proceed down and before we go down one, we want to make sure that it's the one that reflects our deepest, our highest aspirations.'

If you want to be really scared, however, consider what Bostrom calls the 'big wild-card': the singularity. As he puts it in his Transhumanism FAQ on his website, 'Some thinkers conjecture that there will be a point in the future when the rate of technological development becomes so rapid that the progress-curve becomes nearly vertical. Within a very brief time (months, days, or even just hours), the world might be transformed almost beyond recognition.' This would happen if artificial intelligence reached the level where it could learn for itself how to improve, and could work so fast, it would learn at an inconceivably fast rate. 'This hypothetical point is referred to as the singularity.'

It's just impossible to predict, and terrifying to imagine, what would be done by an artificial intelligence that evolved in minutes far beyond the capabilities we have achieved after 50,000 years. In conversation, Bostrom says there is 'some plausibility' to the school of thought which says that, in such a scenario, 'what would happen would be an existential catastrophe, almost certainly, unless it had been designed with exquisite care, in the light of some theoretical understanding that we don't yet possess'.

I'm not sure what to make of all this, but I am sure that we don't take transhumanism seriously enough. It's easy to dismiss superintelligence, uploading and cryogenics as distant possibilities and ignore the lesser technologies which really do look likely to start making an impact on who and what we are in the relatively near future. For that reason, it is worrying that Bostrom admits, 'It is true though that in transhumanist thinking in general and certainly in my own thinking in particular, there hasn't been a great deal of attention so far given to the question of what concept of personal identity would be most appropriate.'

So far, the vast majority of thinking about what we are as persons has been an attempt at description. I think we now have a fairly comprehensive understanding of what we are. You and I are what our bodies and brains do. There is no pearl sitting at the core of our selves, we are rather bundles of psychosomatic activity, albeit highly organised and remarkably stable ones. We are not illusions but we are not what we most obviously appear to be either. The picture may not be entirely complete and some questions remain, but more than two millennia of philosophy, a century of modern psychology and fifty years of neuroscience have given us a clear enough picture of what it means to be a person.

However, we are moving now to a time when questions of *prescription* are becoming much more important. The most important question from here on is different: what do we *want* it to mean to be a person? The question has an urgency because we are already able to fashion the self in much more radical ways than our ancestors ever could, and in this respect we are about to get even more powerful. To paraphrase Marx, until now the philosophers have only interpreted the self; the point now is how, if at all, to change it.

'I no longer get the illusion of free will.'

Susan Blackmore, psychologist

12

Living without a soul

'My life seemed like a glass tunnel, through which I was moving faster every year, and at the end of which there was darkness. When I changed my view, the walls of my glass tunnel disappeared. I now live in the open air.'[1]

These are not the kinds of words you typically read in contemporary anglophone analytic philosophy. But there they are, in Derek Parfit's *Reasons and Persons*, describing the effect of adopting his version of the bundle theory. And why shouldn't such a shift of philosophical theory be life changing? On the pearl view, life can indeed seem like a narrow tube down which we are dropped, accelerating all the time as the years shorten with age, the end approaching with alarming rapidity. But on the bundle view, the hardness of both tube and pearl disappear. The boundaries of the self become vaguer. 'There is still a difference between my life and the lives of other people,' writes Parfit. 'But the difference is less.'

However, many people are baffled by Parfit's rhapsodic declaration. Agreeing with Wittgenstein, they believe philosophy 'leaves everything as it is'. The goal of philosophy is not a kind of transformative enlightenment, but simply better understanding. The epiphany of the philosopher is not 'I see the light!' but, 'Ahhh, I see . . .'

As is so often the case, the truth lies somewhere in between. Accepting a bundle view of the self can make a significant difference to our understanding of free will, how we consider the relationship between self and other and, maybe, how we anticipate the prospect of death. But it perhaps makes not quite as dramatic a difference as you might think, considering the radical remodelling of the self it entails. As the philosopher Daniel Dennett told me, 'This is the nature of philosophy: that the transformations that are legitimate are always in one sense subtle and in another sense very important. After all, what could be more important than, for instance, utterly jettisoning the idea of an immortal soul that might go to heaven or hell. Poof! Gone. But life goes on and you still have a soul – it's just not *that*.'

Free will

Even if you have not been entirely convinced by my argument, I would hope that most readers have at least accepted that whatever you are, you function because your brain and body function and there's no other extra thing that is *you,* sitting inside handling the controls.

There are problems for the notion of free will regardless of any particular view of the self. But if you accept anything like a bundle theory, one problem becomes extremely acute. If who you are and what you do is simply the result of your brain and body function, and your brain and body are part of the physical world, subject to physical laws, aren't all your thoughts and actions just the products of natural forces? Your actions may be more complicated and varied than those of a plant, but your opening of a book is no more free from scientific laws of cause and effect than the opening of a flower.

Many people find this suggestion outrageous. Of course, it doesn't *feel* like this. It seems to us that whenever we make a choice, we could have chosen otherwise. If I'm in a cafe and order an espresso, I feel that I could have ordered a cappuccino instead. But is that true? Not according to the theory known as determinism: in any unique combination of me and an environment, *at the point of action* I am going to act in one way and one way only. Given my preferences, which are a product of my inherited nature and my life experience, given the options available, given how much money I have, given how hungry and thirsty I feel, and so on, it is inevitable which drink I'll choose. That is not to say it is necessarily *predictable*. The combination of causal factors is so complicated that it is often impossible to predict human choice with any accuracy. But do not confuse unpredictability with freedom. Chaos theory explains why many complex systems like the weather are unpredictable, but that does not mean clouds have free will.

That's why the idea critical to the free will debate – that *we could have done otherwise* – is far from straightforward. In one way, determinism does not deny this. We are a long way from the old-fashioned deterministic view of Laplace, the French mathematician, who wrote: 'Given for one instant an intelligence which could comprehend all the forces by which nature is animated and the respective situation of the beings that compose it – an intelligence sufficiently vast to submit these data to analysis – it would embrace in the same formula the movements of the greatest bodies of the universe and those of the lightest atom; for it, nothing would be uncertain and the future, as the past, would be present to its eyes.'[2] On this view, the universe, and the people in it, are like clockwork mechanisms, all of whose future actions are in theory predictable, for ever.

Chaos theory and quantum theory show, in different ways, why this is false. If it starts raining tomorrow at 15:07:43, that is not because it was always going to start raining at that time. The weather could have been otherwise. But, still, the weather that does happen is produced by nothing more than physical systems behaving according to natural laws, and at 15:07:42 it is as good as certain that it will start raining one second later. At that point, the weather could not have done otherwise.

So if we return to the cafe, it is in one sense true that there is nothing inevitable about my choice of espresso. The world could have unfolded differently and I might have found myself ordering the cappuccino instead. But having got to that point, determinism says I could not have chosen otherwise. My decision issued from a psychosomatic system that was in a particular state in a particular environment and, being a physical system, it could only, at that point, have acted one way. Even if quantum effects mean this is not strictly true, all that adds is an element of randomness, not choice.

Given what we know about brains, bodies and actions, determinism looks as if it must be true. There is nothing more to us than a psychosomatic system, which operates according to physical laws, in a physical environment. There may be other theoretical possibilities, but they don't even get off the ground, if we accept the kind of bundle theory I'm advocating. The most notable alternative is voluntarism, which states that our free choices originate in some internal act of will which is not in any way simply a result of the processing of socially situated, embodied brains. Whatever the merits of this theory – and a recent survey of professional philosophers and graduate students suggested that fewer than one in five accepted it – it just isn't available to someone who adopts the broad view of the self I have outlined.[3]

If acceptance of some kind of determinism is required by the bundle theory, how on earth do you live with it? Doesn't it mean giving up a fundamental belief about our own freedom? It does, but that may not be as catastrophic as it sounds. The neuroscientist David Eagleman imagines an afterlife in which you see for yourself the mathematical code that determines all your actions. Shocked, you wonder, 'Is love simply an operation of the math?' You ask yourself if this is hell or heaven, and the answer turns out to be: both. 'Isn't it wonderful to understand the code?' whisper angelic rewarders, out to convince you that you have attained a kind of celestial enlightenment. 'Does understanding the mechanics of attraction suck all the life of it?' taunt demonic tormentors. But neither demon nor angel has any effect: 'knowing the code does not diminish its pleasure on our tongue' and 'glimpsing the mechanics of love does not alter its intoxicating appeal'.[4]

Eagleman dramatises the common belief that determinism may be true, but we cannot live as though it is true. What we know about the mechanics behind action cannot change the fundamental nature of how it feels to act. Others, however, disagree. Take Susan Blackmore, whose research as a psychologist and thirty years of Zen practice have led her to embrace the bundle view. The issue of free will, she points out, is not the same as the issue of personal identity, but 'it's very much bound up with it because most people, when they talk about free will, feel as though it's *me* who has it. So it is really a self issue.'

For Blackmore, this aspect of the question is particularly important because she is the kind of bundle theorist who claims 'there isn't any continuing self in there', which raises the question, 'who's having this free will?' For this and other reasons, she's been convinced since at least her early twenties that free will is an illusion. Many think that if that's true, it's an illusion we cannot help but fall for. But Blackmore disagrees. 'I've been at it so long that I no longer get the illusion of free will.' That is so, even though she still sometimes has to make difficult decisions.

'Let me give you an example,' she explains. 'I was in bed this morning thinking about this. A few years ago I decided I was not going to fly any more, for environmental reasons. I failed. I have flown a few times since then and I finally decided I'd do one flight a year. That way I can just do the occasionally fantastic things. I've just been invited to go to James Randi's The Amazing Meeting in Las

Vegas, which I've never been to, everyone says it's wonderful, there would be 1,200 people there listening to me talking about whatever it is, and it would be a lot of fun. On the other hand you can't imagine a carbon footprint worse than going to Las Vegas or contributing to a city that is doing such destructive things. So this is an agonising moral, intellectual, personal decision. So up comes a little voice in my head saying "She will make a decision. Let the process go on. Don't interfere. Let the thinking go on: thinking about these issues, thinking about carbon footprints and the poor Colorado river, thinking about the pleasure of giving a lecture to all those people. Just let it go on because a decision will emerge."

'It's not that I have free will. It's that this body here is a decision-making instrument and it will make decisions, given its necessity to do so and its ability to do so. Now that is quite a different way of living. I've given you there quite a big example, but it's the same with the example of: shall I have tea or coffee, or what shall we have for lunch, or shall I go to that party or not, shall I buy that book, what shall I give my daughter for her birthday – all of those things, I, this thing, approaches with a "Well, she will decide."'

With all due consistency, Blackmore applies this thinking to other people as well. 'When I see people doing horrible things which I'm angry about, then I think through similar kinds of things: they're just like me, they're just an organism, they're just something that's been brought up with the environment they have, with the pressures they have, with the abilities they have – they are making these decisions and doing these out of all chance and necessity, as Monod would have said.'

Blackmore realises that many people find this way of thinking not just incomprehensible, but reprehensible. 'That's heartless,' she screams, mimicking the hysterical tone of such a challenge, 'it takes all the humanity and love out of everything! How can you love people and be a human being if you think they're just machines?

'Well, I don't know but I feel actually more able to be compassionate to people by simply seeing them as machines making decisions out of necessity and the environment that they're in. Somehow I become more one with them. I'm just the same as them – we're all in it together.'

Blackmore's response is very much informed by her practice of Zen. The Buddhist traditions all encourage a certain detachment from thoughts and feelings, so that we become mindful of their arising but don't necessarily identify with them as integral parts of ourselves. As Blackmore says, this does not mean that we cannot make decisions, or that we reduce ourselves to mere machines. However, it is not the only way to make determinism palatable. More popular in the western philosophical tradition is a stance known as compatibilism. This accepts the broad determinist point but argues that, nonetheless, some valuable kind of free will does remain.

Compatibilist free will is best understood by asking what we mean in ordinary speech when we say a person has acted freely. Free choices include getting married, cheating on your spouse and ordering an espresso. The acts we call unfree include doing something under the influence of hypnosis, going into a forced marriage or handing over your money to a highwayman. The difference between these two kinds of acts has nothing to do with what is going on in the brain or theories of physical determinism. The difference is that we perform the first set of actions unimpeded or uncoerced, while the second are performed under duress or coercion. In simplest terms, the compatibilist position is that freedom is not the ability to do other than what you actually do, but simply the ability to do whatever it is you choose to do. Whether those choices are simply the products of brains and bodies following the laws of nature or not is beside the point. Indeed, it could be asked, what else could these choices be the products of? Of course we are organic machines, operating according to the laws of nature. Whoever thought we were anything else?

When, for *The Philosophers' Magazine*, I consulted a number of leading philosophers a few years back for their views on what the great intractable issues of our day were, free will was firmly in the top three. What I have said here is clearly not enough to settle the issue. However, what I think should be clear is that bundle theorists can and do happily live with determinism. Whether you reject free will as an illusion, as Susan Blackmore does, or accept a compatibilist view of what freedom really means, the believer in the Ego Trick is not condemned to live life feeling like a passive cog in the machinery of nature.

Freedom, if it is to mean anything, cannot be about being fundamentally separate from the chain of cause and effect that runs through the whole of nature. To understand freedom, you need to understand what it is supposed to contrast with. Many have assumed its opposite is necessity, but if that's right, we have no freedom. It is better to see its opposite as coercion. Perhaps it would be even better if instead of talking about freedom we talked about autonomy. The autonomous person is one who is able to regulate his or her own behaviour based more on the internal machinations of their brains than the winds and tides of external events. The fact that physical machinations nonetheless lie at the root of all we say or do is beside the point. Freedom, like the self, is something to be cultivated from the soil of flesh and blood.

Self and other

One of the most striking claims made by Derek Parfit is: 'There is still a difference between my life and the lives of other people. But the difference is less.' It sounds strange, but the logic behind the claim is clear and compelling. For Parfit, a person is simply a highly ordered and complex network of psychological connections and continuities. But if you ask yourself what we are connected to and continuous with, the answer includes many things that are not inside our own bodies. These include not only other people, but other things.

Many thinkers have had this general idea in different ways. Erving Goffman wrote, 'The store is, in a sense, a part of the pharmacist.'[5] Todd Feinberg says, 'Whenever we identify with another person . . . we partially merge with another person's mind.'[6] William James wrote that 'The old saying that the human person is composed of three parts – soul, body and clothes – is more than a joke. We so appropriate our clothes and identify ourselves with them that there are few of us who, if asked to choose between having a beautiful body clad in raiment perpetually shabby and unclean, and having an ugly and blemished form always spotlessly attired, would not hesitate a moment before making a decisive reply.'[7]

This is not so far from common sense as it might seem. Even popular songs express similar ideas. 'Every time you go away,' sang Paul Young, 'you take a piece of me with you.' The feeling is achingly familiar. The people we are really close to become so deeply part of our lives that they do, in a real sense, become part of our selves. It is common for people to describe the loss of a loved one as like having a part of them ripped out, and the hole that's left sometimes never heals. Douglas Hofstadter talks about losing his wife in similar terms, in a way which is both heartfelt and scientifically rigorous. Hofstadter is another kind of bundle theorist, who thinks we are 'strange loops', not things, but patterns of information that feed back on themselves to create higher, more complex networks of abstraction. 'It ain't the meat, it's the motion,' he colourfully says of the brain's role in identity.[8] But if we are patterns of thought, then other people's patterns can start to be mirrored in our own brains. We internalise their ways of thinking and in that sense parts of them live in us. There is not 'an unbridgeable gap between two such people. Each of them is instead spread out into the other one, and each of them lives partially in the other.'[9] This even provides for a kind of impermanent afterlife. Like an eclipsed sun, 'when someone dies, they leave a glowing corona behind them, an afterglow in the souls of those who were close to them . . . When, eventually, all those close ones have died as well, then all the embers will have gone cold, and at that last point, it's "ashes to ashes and dust to dust".'[10]

Perhaps the most respectable and well-developed recent version of this view is the extended-mind thesis, developed by the philosophers David Chalmers and Andy Clark. 'The key idea is that when bits of the environment are hooked up to your cognitive system in the right way, they are, in effect, part of the mind, part of the cognitive system,' explained Chalmers when I spoke to him at the 2008 World Congress of Philosophy in Seoul.[11] 'So, say I'm rearranging Scrabble tiles on a rack. This is very close to being analogous to the situation when I'm doing an anagram in my head. In one case the representations are out in the world, in the other case they're in here. We say doing an anagram on a rack ought to be regarded as a cognitive process, a process of the mind, even though it's out there in the world.'

Taken to its logical conclusion, that means Chalmers' iPhone 'can be seen literally as a part of my mind. I actually remember things by virtue of this information being in the iPhone, it is part of my memory. So the extended-mind thesis basically says that the iPhone isn't just a tool for my cognition, it's part of my cognition.'

The extended-mind thesis may be overstated, but something like it becomes almost inevitable once you reject the pearl view of self. 'The very strongly Cartesian view of the self is that it is just an internal conscious core. But the conscious core is just a very discontinuous thing. It disappears when you go to sleep, it's changing constantly, and so on. To get continuity you've really got to go outside of consciousness to the elements of character and personality, which drive the conscious core. And it turns out that many of those stable things may also be present in the environment. If my iPhone's always around me, if my notebook's always around me, then just as my memories

227

will be part of who I am, my iPhone and my notebook might well be part of who I am.' The obvious objection that you can lose your phone or notebook in a second but not whole stores of memories is sadly disconfirmed by numerous cases of brain injury.

We've seen time and again how the bundle theory opens up all sorts of amazing-sounding possibilities that on closer inspection turn out to be far less radical. Talk of the dissolving of walls between self and other could very easily go the same way. While it is incontrovertible that the bundle view requires us to give up the idea of the self having a sharp, determinate boundary, the extent to which persons interpenetrate each other and the world is surely extremely limited. The vast majority of the psychological connections and continuities that make up the self are internal to our own minds, our own brains, our own bodies. People do 'live on' in the minds of loved ones, but only in a vastly diminished sense, traces left by shadows long after the sun has set.

Nevertheless, it does mean something to recognise the porous boundaries of the self. It is all part and parcel of seeing oneself as less solid and determinate. For me, this does make some difference. Getting used to the idea that I am a process, never remaining the same, helps me to accept how life too is forever in flux, never settled for too long. Accepting the impermanence of self is part of accepting the impermanence of all things. Parfit is right: there is still a difference between my life and the lives of other people, as there is between land and sea. That difference, however, is now more like a tidal beach, and less like a cliff edge.

Death

There is an old saying that there are no atheists in foxholes. People may say they believe that death is the end and there is no God, but when oblivion is staring them in the face, they'll hang on to whatever hope they can, and pray to whoever might be listening.

I find this claim bizarre for three very different reasons. Even if it were true, I'm not sure what it's supposed to prove other than the fact that people will believe anything if desperate. It wouldn't show that atheists are insincere, only that they are human and weak. Second, it's just factually false. We have countless testimonies from atheists who have faced what seemed like certain death and who did not reach for the divine. Indeed, brushes with death often have the effect of making people cherish mortal life more, rather than lean more heavily on the prospect of a life to come.

But third, it seems that the charge can be turned around: there are no theists at funerals. Many people say that they believe that death is not the end, but the way people behave at graveyards and crematoria suggests that they don't really believe it. You may cry and be upset at the prospect of a long separation from someone you love. But I don't think that's how death feels to most people. The parting feels absolute and final.

The very language of death seems to confirm this. We talk of 'loss', without any mention of the prospect of finding again. The most common inscription on a Christian tombstone is 'Rest In Peace', which sounds reassuring but, like the phrase 'merely sleeping', suggests a cessation of all that we would normally associate with life. There is no awakening from eternal sleep, so falling into it is as final a full stop as anything could be. There is nothing 'mere' about such ceaseless slumber.

Beliefs about what follows life can alter how we respond to death, but it seems that the vast majority of human beings at all times and all places react to the deaths of loved ones in ways which only make sense if at some level they really did think that was the end. This is perhaps a rare heartening example of the inability of obvious falsehoods to really convince, even when most people officially believe them.

If the boundaries of the self are blurred, does that not mean that death becomes less a full stop and more an ellipsis? Parfit suggests so.

Before he embraced a bundle view, he thought: 'After my death, there will be no one living who is me.' This remains true, but he can now redescribe it in a way that 'seems to me less bad'. Although 'there will later be many experiences, none of these experiences will be connected to my present experiences by chains of such direct connection as those involving experience-memory, or in the carrying out of an earlier intention . . . My death will break the more direct relations between my present experiences and future experiences, but it will not break various other relations.'[12]

I must admit that seems to me less bad only in the way that having all but two of your teeth punched out isn't as bad as being left with just one. As I have argued, we may be 'just' bundles, but these bundles are incredibly well organised. Although fragile and loose in some ways, they are very highly unified and coherent in others. Like a complicated model made of stacked cards, the organisation is all. If they topple over, plenty remains, but the model itself most certainly does not.

There are, of course, numerous classic arguments as to why we should not fear death. Many of the most enduring, however, do not depend on taking any particular view of the self, other than that it is mortal. Marcus Aurelius, for instance, often encouraged us to look at things from the perspective of the universe. What then happens is that our own lives become so small and insignificant that whether we live or die or not no longer matters much. 'If a God were to tell you, "Tomorrow, or at best the day after, you will be dead," you would not, unless the most abject of men, be greatly solicitous, whether it was to be the later day, rather than the morrow – for what is the difference between them? In the same way, do not reckon it of great moment, whether it will come years and years hence, or tomorrow.'[13]

Another traditional comfort for the mortal is that there's no point worrying about being dead, because when you're dead you won't be there to have anything to worry about. Or, as Epicurus more poetically put it, 'Death is nothing to us, since when we exist, death is not present to us, and when death is present, we have no existence.'[14]

Compared to these, the idea that some psychological connections and continuities persist after death is scant consolation. Indeed, none of the other secular bundle theorists I talked to went as far as Parfit did. Nonetheless, in more subtle ways, they did illustrate how perhaps holding a bundle theory can alter your perception of death.

Paul Broks, for instance, says that 'If anything, it's made me more of a present-oriented person.' You might say that any view of the self that rejects life after death would have the same effect, since it would force us to make the most of the life we have or fall into despair. But there are two ways in which holding a bundle theory might change how we choose to make the most of the one life we have.

First, it is not the same to focus on our mortal lives as a whole as it is to focus on the time around the present. Someone may be convinced that they are mortal and yet not live for the day, the week or even the year. They may live for the whole life, building for a comfortable retirement, for instance. Pearl theories may reinforce that, because they create the illusion that there is no essential difference between retired-you and just-graduated you. It therefore makes rational sense to worry as much about what happens in thirty years as it does what happens in thirty minutes. On a bundle view, the greater the distance in time, the weaker the unity. Although it may be irrational to care nothing at all about what will happen in thirty years' time, it may be entirely rational to care less about it than the more immediate, strongly connected future.

Second, seizing the day can be a rather desperate, tragic affair, especially if you do so only because the alternative is not available. *Carpe diem* becomes the consolation prize for those who would rather *carpe aeternitatem*: seize eternity. The bundle theory, however, shows that *carpe aeternitatem* is beyond us, even if we could be made immortal. Persons do not have a sufficiently fixed and constant nature to persist long enough to even seize a millennium, let alone eternity. You could stop your body dying but you could not stop your self changing, so that, in time, your current self would in effect have been superseded by another one, so far removed from you that he was as little connected and continuous with you now as you are with a long-dead relation. That is why the bundle theorist's rejection of the afterlife is not just an acceptance of the harsh facts of biological reality, but an acceptance that we are not the kinds of beings who are made for eternity.

Stephen Batchelor is another bundle theorist who has learned to embrace his mortality, having no 'great fear of death' nor a 'hankering for some continuity after death. To see the self as a contingent impermanent process is in a sense a recognition that death is simply part of that. Who I am is unintelligible apart from the notion that I will cease, that what I am is something that is moving inexorably towards its end. To live fully is to embrace that fact, to take every moment as an opportunity, as something quite precious, as something that will not last. To me it has an aesthetic consequence.

'If you try to deny death you're also denying life, in a way. You are refusing to accept what is fundamental to your condition as a person: that you are dying all the time, you are dissolving, you're failing; potentially you could flicker out at any moment.'

However, if you accept life's impermanence and value it even more for its finitude, why should that make you any less concerned by death? I'm reminded of a remark by the author Terry Pratchett: 'I think I'm probably an atheist, but rather angry with God for not existing.' In the same way, I believe death is the end, but I'm angry with the universe for making life so short, and its end so capriciously unpredictable. The Buddhist prescription to ease this anger, one which is readily secularised, is to weaken our *tanhā*: sometimes translated as 'attachment' but better understood as 'grasping'. As Batchelor puts it, 'You can only be attached to something you already have,' and so if we don't have a solid, persisting self, we are wrong to think ourselves attached to it.

'The self in some ways, in its more neurotic aspects, as something fixed, is basically a crystallisation of a certain craving, a certain grasping. It's like if you tighten your fist very very tight you will get to a point where it feels like it is a kind of solid thing, whereas in fact it's not. And as you release your grasp, the hand is still just as much there but now it's able to do all sorts of stuff and it doesn't feel solidified in the same way. What Buddhism is interested in is degrasping, it's a letting go, it's a releasing of this tight clutch on to things which actually is life denying.'

Although it is surely right to say that we are often too attached to the wrong things, it seems to me that some attachments are central to life, and to try to weaken them is to diminish what matters most. I think, for example, of my partner. By Buddhist standards, my attachment to her is pathological. We are setting ourselves up for the most horrendous inserenity if, as is almost inevitable, one of us dies before the other. But that is a price we are willing to pay. The alternative is almost inhuman. And it certainly seems to me that thinking of her as a bundle does not make me any less attached to her.

'Or more so even,' agrees Susan Blackmore. 'I certainly think of Adam, whom I love deeply, as a biological machine. He's a sixty-something-year-old man, somewhat overweight with high blood pressure, he could die at any moment. I do actively remind myself that that could happen. I mustn't assume he's going to be around with me for the next twenty to thirty years. I would love him to be, so if he dies I will be devastated, I will cope. None of that changes.'

And for all that the bundle view does, in some ways, radically change how you view life, self, free will and others, in this, as in many other situations, it does seem that holding a bundle view leaves more as it is than it changes.

'I think that's true,' agrees Blackmore. 'I think what has happened to me at least is, you think these things are going to be really, really difficult and dramatic, and you fear making the change, and it really is quite difficult to make the change, because you're stuck in ways of thinking you've inherited from our language and culture and everything else. Once you do it, you find it doesn't actually change everything in your life. You go on doing the same kinds of things, you go on doing your job, cooking the dinner, whatever it is, and actually not that much has changed. But how do you measure amounts of change? There are different kinds of change we're talking about. In some sense, something deep has shifted, and in other senses life carries on as it was.'

Of course, the person I most wanted to ask about the liberating effects of embracing a bundle theory was Derek Parfit, to whose work in this area my PhD was really just a series of footnotes. Parfit doesn't give interviews, but we did have an unrecorded conversation over lunch at All Souls College, Oxford, and in a series of subsequent emails – from which I have already quoted – he did write one thing that seemed to differ from the sentiments expressed in the glass-tunnel passage: 'I wouldn't expect acceptance of "the true view" to have great transformative powers, chiefly because the true view is so hard to accept.' The pearl view has become so deep-rooted that we cannot see that it deserves to be cast before swine after all. Messy, complicated, amorphous bundles are more remarkable and more human than cold, hard gems.

Acknowledgements

First and foremost, I must thank the many people who spared their time to be interviewed for this book: Stephen Batchelor, Janet Bell, Susan Blackmore, Nick Bostrom, Paul Broks, Rita Carter, Aubrey de Grey, Jñanamitra, Brooke Magnanti, Drusilla Marland, Derek Parfit, Akong Tulku Rinpoche, Ringu Tulku Rinpoche, Jackie Smith, Galen Strawson, Richard Swinburne, Justin Thacker and Philip Zimbardo. I am especially grateful to Robert and Linda, which, for reasons of confidentiality, are not their real names. Although I didn't quote from it, an early interview with Norman Hansen was also extremely useful. I also interviewed David Chalmers, Dan Dennett and Susan Greenfield officially for other purposes, but hijacked some of the time for this project.

In addition, I also received help and guidance from Stephen Cave, Cheryl McElroy, Simon Stuart, Barbara Tomenson and Ben Whalley.

Ophelia Benson, Sara Holloway, Lizzy Kremer and Antonia Macaro all provided invaluable comments on the first draft of this book, thanks to which I hope this one is significantly better.

I am grateful to everyone who has worked at or for Granta to make this book as good and successful as possible, in particular Benjamin Buchan, Stephen Guise, Christine Lo, Brigid Macleod, Sharon Murphy, Aidan O'Neill, Kelly Pike, Angela Rose, Pru Rowlandson and Sarah Wasley.

Finally, I should thank Michael Proudfoot, whose undergraduate lectures got me interested in the subject in the first place, and Lucy O'Brien, who supervised the PhD which is the seed out of which this very different book grew.

Bibliography

Aurelius, Marcus, *Meditations*, trans. Maxwell Staniforth (London: Penguin, 1964)

Austin, J.L., *Sense and Sensibilia* (Oxford: Oxford University Press, 1962)

Barresi, John, 'On Becoming a Person', *Philosophical Psychology*, vol. 12, no. 1 (1999), pp. 79–98

Bayley, John, *Iris: A Memoir of Iris Murdoch* (London: Abacus, 1999)

Beard, Richard, *Becoming Drusilla* (London: Harvill Secker, 2008)

Belle de Jour [Brooke Magnanti], *Belle's Best Bits* (London: Orion, 2010)

Bennett, M.R. and Hacker, P.M.S., *Foundations of Neuroscience* (Oxford: Blackwell, 2003)

Bratman, Michael E., 'Reflection, Planning and Temporally Extended Agency', *The Philosophical Review*, vol. 109, no. 1 (January 2000), pp. 35–61

Braun, K.A., Ellis, R. and Loftus, E.F., 'Make my Memory: How Advertising can Change our Memories of the Past', *Psychology and Marketing*, 19 (2002), pp. 1–23

Broks, Paul, *Into the Silent Land* (London: Atlantic Books, 2003)

Brown, Warren S., Murphy, Nancey and Malony, H. Newton (eds), *Whatever Happened to the Soul? Scientific and Theological Portraits of Human Nature* (Minneapolis: Fortress Press, 1998)

Buñuel, Luis, *My Last Sigh* (Minneapolis: University of Minnesota Press, 2003)

Butler, Christopher, *Postmodernism: A Very Short Introduction* (Oxford: Oxford University Press, 2002)

Carter, Rita, *Multiplicity: The New Science of Personality* (London: Little, Brown, 2008)

Cassam, Quassim, *Self and World* (Oxford: Oxford University Press, 1997)

Christensen, K., Doblhammer, G., Rau, R. and Vaupel, J., 'Ageing

Bibliography

Populations: The Challenges Ahead', *The Lancet*, vol. 374, issue 9696 (3 October 2009), pp. 1196–1208

Dainton, Barry, 'The Self and the Phenomenal', *Ratio* (new series), vol. XVII, no. 4 (December 2004), pp. 365–89

Damasio, Antonio, *The Feeling of What Happens: Body, Emotion and the Making of Consciousness* (London: Heinemann, 2000)

Darley, J.M. and Batson, C.D., 'From Jerusalem to Jericho: A Study of Situational and Dispositional Variables in Helping Behaviour', *Journal of Personality and Social Psychology*, 27 (1973), pp. 100–108

Descartes, René, *Meditations on First Philosophy*, trans. John Cottingham (Cambridge: Cambridge University Press, 1986 [1641])

Diogenes Laertius, *The Lives and Opinions of Eminent Philosophers*, trans. C.D. Yonge (London: Henry G. Bohn, 1853)

Doris, John M., *Lack of Character* (Cambridge: Cambridge University Press, 2002)

Eagleman, David, *Sum: Forty Tales from the Afterlives* (Edinburgh: Canongate, 2009)

Faludi, Susan, *The Terror Dream: What 9/11 Revealed about America* (London: Atlantic, 2008)

Feinberg, Todd E., *Altered Egos: How the Brain Creates the Self* (New York: Oxford University Press, 2001)

Feinberg, Todd E., *From Axons to Identity* (New York: W.W. Norton, 2009)

Feinberg, Todd E. and Keenan, Julian Paul (eds), *The Lost Self: Pathologies of Brain and Identity* (Oxford: Oxford University Press, 2005)

Forer, B.R., 'The Fallacy of Personal Validation: A Classroom Demonstration of Gullibility', *Journal of Abnormal and Social Psychology* (American Psychological Association), 44 (1), 1949, pp. 118–23

Frankfurt, Harry G., 'Freedom of the Will and the Concept of a Person', *The Journal of Philosophy*, vol. 68, no. 1 (January 1971), pp. 5–20

Fricker, Miranda and Hornsby, Jennifer (eds), *The Cambridge Companion to Feminism in Philosophy* (Cambridge: Cambridge University Press, 2000)

Gazzaniga, Michael S., *Human: The Science Behind What Makes Us Unique* (New York: Ecco, 2008)

Goffman, Erving, *The Presentation of Self in Everyday Life* (Harmondsworth: Penguin, 1969 [1959])

Greenfield, Susan, *ID: The Quest for Identity in the 21st Century* (London: Sceptre, 2008)

Guilbert, Georges-Claude, *Madonna as Postmodern Myth: How One Star's Self-construction Rewrites Sex, Gender, Hollywood and the American Dream* (Jefferson, North Carolina: McFarland & Co., 2002)

Harré, Rom, 'Persons and Selves,' in *Persons and Personality*, ed. Arthur Peacocke and Grant Gillet (Oxford: Basil Blackwell, 1987)

Hilts, Philip J., *Memory's Ghost: The Nature of Memory and the Strange Case of Mr M* (New York: Touchstone, 1996)

Hobbes, Thomas, *Hobbes' English Works* ,volume 1, ed. Sir W. Molesworth (London: John Bohn, 1839)

Hofstadter, Douglas, *I Am a Strange Loop* (New York: Basic Books, 2007)

Hume, David, *A Treatise of Human Nature*, Book 1 (London: Fontana, 1962 [1739])

Humphry, Nicholas and Dennett, Daniel C., 'Speaking for Our Selves: An Assessment of Multiple Personality Disorder', *Raritan*, 9:1 (1989), pp. 68–98

Husserl, Edmund, *Cartesian Meditations* (The Hague: Martinus Nijhoff, 1950)

Isen, A.M. and Levin, P.F., 'Effects of Feeling Good on Helping: Cookies and Kindness', *Journal of Personality and Social Psychology*, 21 (1972), pp. 384–8

James, Susan, 'Feminism in Philosophy of Mind: The Question of Personal Identity', in Fricker and Hornsby (2000)

James, William, *The Principles of Psychology*, vol. 1 (New York: Dover Books, 1950 [1890])

Jinpa, Thupten, *Self, Reality and Reason in Tibetan Philosophy: Tsongkhapa's Quest for the Middle Way* (Oxford: RoutledgeCurzon, 2002)

Judt, Tony, 'Night', *New York Review of Books*, vol. 57, no. 1 (14 January 2010)

Kant, Immanuel, *The Critique of Pure Reason*, trans. Norman Kemp Smith (London: Macmillan, 1933 [1781])

Kierkegaard, Søren, *Stages on Life's Way*, trans. W. Lowrie (Oxford: Oxford University Press, 1940 [1845])

Korsgaard, Christine M., 'Personal Identity and the Unity of Agency: A Kantian Response to Parfit', *Philosophy and Public Affairs*, vol. 18, no. 2 (Spring 1989), pp. 101–32; reprinted in Martin and Barresi (2003)

Bibliography

Korsgaard, Christine M., *Self-Constitution: Agency, Identity, and Integrity* (Oxford: Oxford University Press, 2009)

Laing, R.D., *The Divided Self* (London: Penguin, 1990 [1959])

Laplace, Pierre Simon, *A Philosophical Essay on Probabilities*, trans. Frederick Wilson Truscott and Frederick Lincoln Emory (New York: John Wiley and Sons, 1902 [1814])

Leibniz, G.W., *Discourse on Metaphysics*, in *Philosophical Texts*, trans. and ed. R.S. Woolhouse and Richard Francis (Cambridge: Cambridge University Press, 1998 [1686])

Lewis, David, 'Survival and Identity' (1976), reprinted in Martin and Barresi (2003)

Lloyd, Genevieve, *The Man of Reason: 'Male' and 'Female' in Western Philosophy*, 2nd edition (London: Routledge, 1993)

Locke, John, *An Essay Concerning Human Understanding*, Book 2 (5th edition, 1706)

Loftus, Elizabeth and Ketcham, Katherine, *Witness for the Defense* (New York: St Martin's Press, 1991)

Luria, A.R., *The Neuropsychology of Memory* (New York: Wiley, 1976)

MacLean, Paul D., *The Triune Brain in Evolution: Role in Paleocerebral Functions* (New York: Plenum Press, 1990)

Macrae, N.C., Milne, A.B. and Bodenhausen, G.V., 'Stereotypes as Energy-saving Devices: A Peek Inside the Cognitive Toolbox', *Journal of Personality and Social Psychology,* 66(1) (1994), pp. 37–47

Martin, Raymond, 'Fission Rejuvenation', *Philosophical Studies*, 80 (1995), pp. 17–40; reprinted in Martin & Barresi (2003)

Martin, Raymond and Barresi, John (eds), *Personal Identity* (Oxford: Blackwell, 2003)

Martin, Raymond and Barresi, John, *The Rise and Fall of Soul and Self: An Intellectual History of Personal Identity* (New York: Columbia University Press, 2006)

Nasr, Seyyed Hossein and Leaman, Oliver (eds), *History of Islamic Philosophy* (London: Routledge, 1996)

Nietzsche, Friedrich, *The Will to Power*, trans. Walter Kaufmann (New York: Vintage, 1968 [1901])

Nisbett, Richard E., *The Geography of Thought: How Asians and Westerners Think Differently . . . and Why* (London: Nicholas Brealey Publishing, 2005)

Noonan, Harold W., 'Animalism versus Lockeanism: A Current Controversy', *The Philosophical Quarterly*, vol. 48, no. 192 (July 1998), pp. 301–18

Olsen, Eric T., 'An Argument for Animalism', in Martin and Barresi (2003)

Oxnam, Robert B., *A Fractured Mind: My Life with Multiple Personality Disorder* (London: Fusion Press, 2006)

Parfit, Derek, *Reasons and Persons* (Oxford: Oxford University Press, 2004)

Perry, John, 'Can the Self Divide?', *The Journal of Philosophy*, vol. 69, no. 16 (September 1972), pp. 463–88

Radcliffe Richards, Janet, *The Sceptical Feminist,* 2nd edition (Harmondsworth: Penguin, 1994)

Ram-Prasad, Chakravarthi, *Eastern Philosophy* (London: Weidenfeld & Nicolson, 2005)

Ratzinger, Joseph Cardinal, *Introduction to Christianity* (San Francisco: Ignatius Press: 2004)

Reid, Thomas, *Essays on the Intellectual Powers of Man* (Cambridge, MA: MIT Press, 1969 [1785])

Ricoeur, Paul, *Oneself as Another*, trans. Kathleen Blamey (Chicago: University of Chicago Press, 1992)

Rovane, Carol, *The Bounds of Agency* (Princeton: Princeton University Press, 1998)

Russell, Bertrand, *The Philosophy of Logical Atomism* (Peru, Illinois: Open Court, 1985 [1918])

Ryle, Gilbert, *The Concept of Mind* (London: Peregrine, 1963 [1949])

Schechtman, Marya, 'Experience, Agency, and Personal Identity', *Social Philosophy and Policy*, vol. 22, issue 2 (July 2005), pp. 1–24

Segal, Suzanne, *Collision with the Infinite*, 2nd edition (San Diego: Blue Dove Press, 1996)

Singer, Peter, *Practical Ethics* (Cambridge: Cambridge University Press, 1979)

Sperry, R.W., 'Brain Bisection and Mechanisms of Consciousness', in J.C. Eccles (ed.), *Brain and Conscious Experience* (Berlin: Springer-Verlag, 1966)

Strawson, Galen, 'The Self', *Journal of Consciousness Studies*, 4:5–6 (1997), pp. 405–428; reprinted in Martin and Barresi (2003) with a new postscript

Bibliography

Strawson, Galen, *Selves* (Oxford: Oxford University Press, 2009)

Swinburne, Richard, *The Evolution of the Soul*, revised edition (Oxford: Oxford University Press, 1997)

White, Thomas I., *In Defense of Dolphins: The New Moral Frontier* (Malden, MA: Wiley-Blackwell, 2007)

Wilkes, Kathleen, *Real People: Personal Identity Without Thought Experiments* (Oxford: Clarendon Press, 1993)

Williams, Bernard, *Problems of the Self* (Cambridge: Cambridge University Press, 1973)

Williams, Bernard, *Truth and Truthfulness: An Essay in Genealogy* (Princeton: Princeton University Press, 2002)

Wittgenstein, Ludwig, *The Blue and Brown Books* (Oxford: Blackwell, 1958)

Wittgenstein, Ludwig, *Philosophical Investigations*, 3rd edition, trans. G.E.M. Anscombe (Oxford: Blackwell, 1967)

Notes

Introduction

1 Luis Buñuel, *My Last Sigh*, p. 252.
2 *Handbook of Self and Identity*, ed. Mark Leary and June Tangey (New York: Guilford Press, 2003), cited by Todd E. Feinberg, *From Axons to Identity*, p. x.

Chapter 1: Bodies of thought

1 Eric T. Olsen, 'An Argument for Animalism', in *Personal Identity*, ed. Raymond Martin and John Barresi, pp. 318–34.
2 John Locke, *An Essay Concerning Human Understanding*, Book 2, chapter 27, section 15.
3 Richard Beard, *Becoming Drusilla*, p. 3.
4 Press Association video, 19 October 2009.
5 Nicky Murfitt, 'I was savagely disfigured by my deranged boyfriend: Acid attack victim bravely shows her face', *Daily Mail*, 19 October 2009.
6 *Katie: My Beautiful Face* (Mentorn Media), first broadcast 29 October 2009, Channel Four.
7 Ed Pilkington, 'A bunch of dead muscles, thinking', *Guardian*, 9 January 2010.
8 Tony Judt, 'Night', *New York Review of Books*, vol. 57, no. 1 (14 January 2010).
9 Ibid.
10 Pilkington, op. cit.
11 Quoted in Susan James, 'Feminism in Philosophy of Mind: The Question of Personal Identity', in Miranda Fricker and Jennifer Hornsby (eds), *The Cambridge Companion to Feminism in Philosophy*, p. 33.

Notes

Chapter 2: Identity on the brain

1 Interview with Suzanne Segal, www.spiritualteachers.org/segal_ interview.htm, accessed 21/01/10.
2 Suzanne Segal, *Collision with the Infinite*, p. 156.
3 Ibid, afterword by Stephan Bodian, p. 174.
4 Ibid, p. 175.
5 Paul D. MacLean, *The Triune Brain in Evolution: Role in Paleocerebral Functions*.
6 Todd E. Feinberg, 'Neural Hierarchies and the Self', in *The Lost Self*, ed. Todd E. Feinberg and Julian Paul Kennan, p. 38.
7 Ibid, p. 39.
8 The most common distinction is the one made famous by Antonio Damasio, who talks about the core and extended self.
9 Todd E. Feinberg, *Altered Egos*, pp. 102–3.
10 Michael S. Gazzaniga, *Human: The Science Behind What Makes Us Unique*, p. 321.
11 Antonio Damasio, *The Feeling of What Happens: Body, Emotion and the Making of Consciousness*, p. 217.

Chapter 3: Memory makers

1 Kathleen Wilkes, *Real People: Personal Identity Without Thought Experiments*.
2 G.W. Leibniz, *Discourse on Metaphysics*, in *Philosophical Texts*, trans. and ed. R.S. Woolhouse and Richard Francis, p. 87.
3 John Locke, *An Essay Concerning Human Understanding*, Book 2, chapter 27, section 9.
4 Raymond Martin and John Barresi, *The Rise and Fall of Soul and Self*, p. 143.
5 As Feinberg (2009) summarises the research, p. 58. See also Esther Fujiwara and Hans J. Markowitsch, 'Autobiographical Disorders', in Feinberg and Keenan (eds), p. 67.
6 Thomas Reid, *Essays on the Intellectual Powers of Man*, Essay 3: 'Of Memory', chapter 6.
7 K.A. Braun, R. Ellis and E.F. Loftus, 'Make my Memory: How

Advertising can Change our Memories of the Past', *Psychology and Marketing*, 19 (2002), pp. 1–23.

8 Elizabeth Loftus and Katherine Ketcham, *Witness for the Defense*, p. 20.

9 Quoted in 'H.M., an Unforgettable Amnesiac, Dies at 82' by Benedict Carey, *New York Times,* 8 December 2008.

10 Philip J. Hilts, *Memory's Ghost: The Nature of Memory and the Strange Case of Mr M.*

11 A.R. Luria, *The Neuropsychology of Memory*, pp. 250–2.

12 John Bayley, *Iris: A Memoir of Iris Murdoch*, p. 294.

13 *Share* (Alzheimer's Society Newsletter), August 2006, pp. 8–9, quote from 'A very poignant love triangle', Frances Hubbard, *Daily Mail*, 7 April 2007.

14 Margaret Jeremiah, letter in *Share*, ibid.

Chapter 4: Soul searching

1 *History of Islamic Philosophy*, ed. Seyyed Hossein Nasr and Oliver Leaman, pp. 315, 1022 and 1023.

2 What seems just as clear is that even if such a fantasy successfully removes any sense of space, time still remains: thinking occurs over time, and I would be very sceptical about anyone who claimed that they could have conscious awareness without any sense of time. When people do report losing a sense of time in meditation, for example, what actually seems to be lost is the normal sense of its speed or progression, not any sense of time at all. So, for instance, on leaving the meditative state, a person may report that they had no idea how long they were in it for, but that does not mean that their experience lacked a linear, extended nature. And if we cannot imagine ourselves outside of time, it could be argued that we implicitly always imagine ourselves in space too, because space and time are not separate dimensions.

3 Gilbert Ryle, *The Concept of Mind*, chapter 1.

4 R.W. Sperry, 'Brain, Bisection and Mechanisms of Consciousness', in J.C. Eccles (ed.), *Brain and Conscious Experience*.

5 David Lewis, 'Survival and Identity', reprinted in *Personal Identity*, ed. Raymond Martin and John Barresi, pp. 144–67.

6 Derek Parfit, *Reasons and Persons*, chapter 12.
7 Richard Swinburne, *The Evolution of the Soul*, pp. 150–51.
8 Derek Parfit, *Reasons and Persons*, p. 210.
9 Swinburne, op. cit., p. 176.
10 Ibid, pp. 310–11.
11 Raymond Martin and John Barresi, *The Rise and Fall of Soul and Self*, p. 83.

Chapter 5: Multiplication

1 Robert B. Oxnam, *A Fractured Mind: My Life with Multiple Personality Disorder*, p. 31.
2 Nicholas Humphry and Daniel C. Dennett, 'Speaking for Our Selves: An Assessment of Multiple Personality Disorder', *Raritan*, 9:1 (1989), pp. 68–98.
3 Oxnam, op. cit., p. 254.
4 Humphry and Dennett, op. cit.
5 Seyla Benhabib, *Situating the Self* (1992), cited in Christopher Butler, *Postmodernism: A Very Short Introduction*.
6 Catherine Belsey, *Critical Practice* (1980), cited in Butler, *Postmodernism*.
7 Bernard Williams, *Truth and Truthfulness*, p. 243.
8 All quotes are from Georges-Claude Guilbert, *Madonna as Postmodern Myth: How One Star's Self-construction Rewrites Sex, Gender, Hollywood and the American Dream*.
9 N.C. Macrae, A.B. Milne and G.V. Bodenhausen, 'Stereotypes as Energy-Saving Devices: A Peek Inside the Cognitive Toolbox', *Journal of Personality and Social Psychology*, 66(1) (1994), pp. 37–47.
10 Ludwig Wittgenstein, *The Blue and Brown Books*, p. 62.
11 See http://astraeasweb.net/plural and www.dreamshore.net/amorpha.
12 Testimony of a co-conscious multiple at http://webspace.webring.com/people/xu/um_10508/multi2.html, accessed 2/4/2010.
13 Rita Carter, *Multiplicity: The New Science of Personality*, p. 49.
14 *The Questions of King Milinda [Milindapañha]*, Part 1, translated by T.W. Rhys Davids, *The Sacred Books of the East,* vol. 35 [1890], Book 2, chapter 1.
15 Friedrich Nietzsche, *The Will to Power*, §§489–490.

Chapter 6: The social self

1 William James, *The Principles of Psychology*, vol. 1, p. 323.
2 William Shakespeare, *As You Like It*, Act 2, Scene 7, ll.139–167.
3 Janet Radcliffe Richards, *The Sceptical Feminist* (2nd edition), p. 64.
4 Erving Goffman, *The Presentation of Self in Everyday Life*, p. 9.
5 Ibid, p. 246.
6 Galen Strawson, *Selves*, p. 26.
7 James, op. cit., p. 336.
8 Rom Harré, 'Persons and Selves,' in *Persons and Personality*, ed. Arthur Peacocke and Grant Gillet.
9 Richard E. Nisbett, *The Geography of Thought: How Asians and Westerners Think Differently . . . and Why*, pp. 90–92.
10 Ibid, p. 121.

Chapter 7: The Ego Trick

1 Bertrand Russell, *The Philosophy of Logical Atomism*, p. 53.
2 John Locke, *An Essay Concerning Human Understanding*, Book 2, chapter 27, para. 13.
3 Peter Singer, *Practical Ethics*, p. 97.
4 Thomas I. White, *In Defense of Dolphins: The New Moral Frontier*.
5 Thomas Reid, *Essays on the Intellectual Powers of Man*, Essay 2: 'Of the Powers we have by means of our External Senses', §12.
6 David Hume, *A Treatise of Human Nature*, Book 1, part 4, section 6.
7 Gilbert Ryle, *The Concept of Mind*, pp. 186–9.
8 Paul Ricoeur, *Oneself as Another*, pp. 137–8.
9 Quassim Cassam, *Self and World*, p. 196.
10 Ibid, p. 2.
11 Antti Revonsuo, 'The Self in Dreams', in *The Lost Self*, ed. Feinberg and Keenan, pp. 209 and 211.
12 Immanuel Kant, *The Critique of Pure Reason*, A363.
13 Galen Strawson, *Selves*, p. 2.
14 Todd E. Feinberg, *From Axons to Identity*, p. 212.
15 Genevieve Lloyd, *The Man of Reason*, p. 4.
16 Quoted in Susan James, 'Feminism in Philosophy of Mind: The Question of Personal Identity', in *The Cambridge Companion to Feminism in Philosophy*, ed. Miranda Fricker and Jennifer Hornsby, p. 33.

17 R.D. Laing, *The Divided Self*, p. 66.
18 René Descartes, *Meditations on First Philosophy*, §81, p. 56.
19 Antonio Damasio, *The Feeling of What Happens: Body, Emotion and the Making of Consciousness*, p. 42.
20 Ibid, pp. 287–8.
21 Thomas Hobbes, *Hobbes' English Works,* volume 1, pp. 135–8.
22 Paul Ricoeur, *Oneself as Another*, p. 116.
23 Ludwig Wittgenstein, *Philosophical Investigations*, §43.
24 Ibid, §71.
25 M.R. Bennett and P.M.S. Hacker, *Foundations of Neuroscience*.
26 Harold W. Noonan, 'Animalism versus Lockeanism: A Current Controversy', *The Philosophical Quarterly*, vol. 48, no. 192 (July 1998), pp. 317–18.
27 Private correspondence, 21/22 May 2010.

Chapter 8: Just an illusion?

1 Chakravarthi Ram-Prasad, *Eastern Philosophy*, p. 58.
2 *Dhammapada*, translated from Pali by F. Max Muller, Project Gutenberg etext, 1 October 2008 [EBook #2017].
3 Thupten Jinpa, *Self, Reality and Reason in Tibetan Philosophy*, pp. 70–71.
4 Paul Ricoeur, *Oneself as Another*, p. 5.
5 J.L. Austin, *Sense and Sensibilia*, p. 26.
6 Douglas Hofstadter, *I Am a Strange Loop*, p. xii.
7 Ibid, pp. 92–3.

Chapter 9: Reconstructing character

1 Paul Ricoeur, *Oneself as Another*, p. 121.
2 See Susan Faludi, *The Terror Dream: What 9/11 Revealed about America*, pp. 55–63.
3 A.M. Isen and P.F. Levin, 'Effects of Feeling Good on Helping: Cookies and Kindness', *Journal of Personality and Social Psychology*, 21 (1972), pp. 384–8.
4 J.M. Darley and C.D. Batson, 'From Jerusalem to Jericho: A Study of Situational and Dispositional Variables in Helping Behaviour', *Journal of Personality and Social Psychology*, 27 (1973), pp. 100–108.

5 John Doris, *Lack of Character*, p. 2.
6 B.R. Forer, 'The Fallacy of Personal Validation: A Classroom Demonstration of Gullibility', *Journal of Abnormal and Social Psychology* (American Psychological Association), 44 (1), 1949, pp. 118–23.
7 Doris, op. cit., pp. 72–3.
8 Christine M. Korsgaard, 'Personal Identity and the Unity of Agency: A Kantian Response to Parfit', reprinted in *Personal Identity*, ed. Raymond Martin and John Barresi, p. 121.
9 Christine M. Korsgaard, *Self-Constitution: Agency, Identity, and Integrity*, p. 130.
10 Ibid, p. 24.
11 Ibid, p. 22.
12 Carol Rovane, *The Bounds of Agency*, p. 24.
13 Marya Schechtman, 'Experience, Agency, and Personal Identity', *Social Philosophy and Policy*, vol. 22, issue 2, July 2005, pp. 1–24 See also Michael E. Bratman, see also 'Reflection, Planning and Temporally Extended Agency', *The Philosophical Review*, vol. 109, no. 1 (January 2000), pp. 35–61.
14 Edmund Husserl, *Cartesian Meditations*, pp. 75 and 66.

Chapter 10: Life after death

1 Warren S. Brown, Nancey Murphy and H. Newton Malony (eds), *Whatever Happened to the Soul? Scientific and Theological Portraits of Human Nature*, p. 215.
2 Thomas Aquinas, *Super epistolas S. Pauli lectorae*, ed. P. Raphaelis Cai (Turin: Marietti, 1953).
3 Joseph Cardinal Ratzinger, *Introduction to Christianity*, p. 347.
4 Ibid, p. 349.
5 Ibid, p. 347.
6 Raymond Martin and John Barresi, *The Rise and Fall of Soul and Self*, p. 126.
7 Brown, Murphy and Malony (eds), *Whatever Happened to Soul?*, p. 11.
8 Joseph Cardinal Ratzinger, op.cit., p. 348.
9 Athenagoras, *Treatise on the Resurrection of the Dead*, trans. Alexander Roberts and James Donaldson, in Peter Kirby, 'Athenagoras of Athens',

Early Christian Writings, 2 February 2006, www.earlychristianwritings. com/athenagoras.html.

10 Brown, Murphy and Malony, op. cit., p. 100.

11 1 Corinthians 15:44 (King James Version).

12 Origen, *On First Principles (De Principiis)*, Book II, chapter 10. Translated by Frederick Crombie, from *Ante-Nicene Fathers*, vol. 4, edited by Alexander Roberts, James Donaldson and A. Cleveland Coxe (Buffalo, NY: Christian Literature Publishing Co., 1885). Revised and edited for New Advent by Kevin Knight, www.newadvent.org/fathers/0412.htm, accessed 05/01/2010.

13 Joseph Cardinal Ratzinger, op.cit., p. 348.

Chapter 11: The future of the self

1 Headlines from the *Daily Mail*, 24 February 2009; the *Guardian*, 24 February 2009; and *The Australian*, 14 June 2008.

2 Roy J. Matthew, 'Psychoactive Agents and the Self', in *The Lost Self*, ed. Feinberg and Keenan, pp. 225 and 233.

3 'Science fact and the SENS agenda: What can we reasonably expect from ageing research?', a rebuttal signed by Huber Warner, Julie Anderson, Steven Austad, Ettore Bergamini, Dale Bredesen, Robert Butler, Bruce A. Carnes, Brian F. C. Clark, Vincent Cristofalo, John Faulkner, Leonard Guarente, David E. Harrison, Tom Kirkwood, Gordon Lithgow, George Martin, Ed Masoro, Simon Melov, Richard A. Miller, S. Jay Olshansky, Linda Partridge, Olivia Pereira-Smith, Tom Perls, Arlan Richardson, James Smith, Thomas von Zglinicki, Eugenia Wang, Jeanne Y. Weil and T. Franklin Williams, *EMBO Reports* 6, 11 (2005), pp.1006–1008.

4 K. Christensen, G. Doblhammer, R. Rau and J. Vaupel, 'Ageing Populations: The challenges Ahead', *The Lancet*, vol. 374, issue 9696 (3 October 2009), pp. 1196–1208.

5 Joe Hicks and Grahame Allen, 'A Century of Change: Trends in UK Statistics since 1900', House of Commons Research Paper 99/111, 21 December 1999.

6 Bernard Williams, 'The Makropulos Case: Reflections on the Tedium of Immortality', in *Problems of the Self*, pp. 82–100.

7 See Nick Bostrom's Transhumanist FAQ at www.nickbostrom.com.

Chapter 12: Living without a soul

1 Derek Parfit, *Reasons and Persons,* p. 281.
2 Pierre Simon Laplace, *A Philosophical Essay on Probabilities*, p. 4.
3 Philpapers surveys, http://philpapers.org/surveys/
4 David Eagleman, *Sum*, pp. 101–3.
5 Erving Goffman, *The Presentation of Self in Everyday Life*, p. 99.
6 Todd E. Feinberg, *From Axons to Identity*, p. 152.
7 William James, *The Principles of Psychology*, vol. 1, p. 292.
8 Douglas Hofstadter, *I Am a Strange Loop*, p. 257.
9 Ibid, p. 272.
10 Ibid, p. 258.
11 Julian Baggini, 'A Piece of iMe: an interview with David Chalmers', *The Philosophers' Magazine*, Issue 43, 4th Quarter 2008, pp. 41–9.
12 Derek Parfit, *Reasons and Persons*, p. 281.
13 Marcus Aurelius, *Meditations,* Book 4, §47, p. 74.
14 Diogenes Laertius, *The Lives and Opinions of Eminent Philosophers*, p. 469.

Index

Index

Index